THE JA BUSTER

Definitions and meanings for the 800
most useful words and phrases in
Associations and Membership Organisations

WE NEED SOME NEW JARGON,
THE STAFF ARE STARTING TO
UNDERSTAND WHAT WE'RE
TALKING ABOUT!

Susie Kay & Richard Gott

COPYRIGHT NOTICE

INTRODUCTION

Too much jargon?

Too confusing for those coming new to the sector?

Too frustrating to those coming back to or moving within the sector?

Too many assumptions that we are all referring to the same thing in our discussions?

If your answer to any of the above questions is 'yes', then this publication is for you and should be kept close at hand to enable some serious 'jargon busting'.

This publication was compiled by Susie Kay from The Professionalism Group and Richard Gott from the MemberWise Network in response to cries for help concerning the sometimes overwhelming use of acronyms and jargon within the membership and association sector.

For example, look at the acronym "CPD" - it looks innocent enough. You might expect to see it defined as 'continuing professional development'. However it takes only a few seconds with a dictionary or glossary to discover that there are a total of 118 different possible meanings including 'community planning and development', 'collaborative product development', 'construction products directive', and 'capabilities production document' amongst many others.

Being based outside the UK will further complicate matters, e.g. "CPD" in the United States could be taken to mean the Chicago Police Department! That's enough to set some significant misunderstandings loose within any organisation.

Staff and stakeholders at all levels will find the simple and straightforward A to Z format of this resource quick and simple to use. Words which begin with a capital letter indicate there is another entry which may assist further. Any terms which have alternate terminology will be defined for the first entry only so follow the link.

The definitions we provide have been derived from a very wide range of sources and quality assured by fellow association and membership professionals. We recognise only too well that acronyms are being created all the time so if you come across one that is not featured please do let us know!

Susie Kay, Managing Director, The Professionalism Group
Richard Gott, Chair, MemberWise Network

January 2015

WHAT DOES THE SECTOR THINK OF THE JARGON BUSTER?

"This book is a great idea. It is the kind of book that's worth having close at hand so you can confidently put your point across in any membership or association conversation at any time. The membership industry is all about being inclusive and if we can help make entering the industry itself even more accessible through demystifying some of the language then we are taking a leaf out of our own book, so to speak. "
Laura Fleming, Head of Membership Engagement, Royal College of Physicians

"Working in the world of membership bodies can seem daunting, given that the sector is unique in many ways and has developed its own set of jargon. This book is an invaluable reference tool, comprehensively and clearly explaining many terms – both general and sector-specific – that you may need to know and understand."
Sara Llewellyn, Head of Internal Communications, ACCA

"A detailed and practical guide for anyone involved with trade associations and professional membership bodies. This is an invaluable resource for those who don't know as well as those who should know, but don't."
Andrew Chalk, Director of Operations, BBSA

"This is a handy and useful book for membership professionals, both new and experienced. Great for a new member of staff who is learning about membership organisations but also good to refer back from time to time. Clear, concise and comprehensive; everything you need from a reference title such as this."
Luke Stevens-Burt, Head of Business Development (Member Services), Chartered Institute of Library and Information Professionals

"I think the guide is really useful, particularly for those new to the association sector."
Vicky Vine, Communications Director, Association of Optometrists

"I think this is very comprehensive – essential for anyone starting out in membership. I love that you included 'Death by Powerpoint …!'
Stephanie R, Head of Membership, science sector institute

A

Academic accreditation

A type of quality assurance process under which services and operation of educational institutions or programmes are evaluated by an external awarding body (the membership organisation or professional association) to determine if applicable standards are met. If standards are met, accredited status is granted by the external body. Alternate forms of accreditation are:

- Corporate accreditation
Accreditation of a corporate entity(ies) or organisation
- Training provider or training course accreditation
Accreditation of a training provider or course

ACAS

The Advisory, Conciliation and Arbitration Service is a Crown non-departmental public body of the Government of the United Kingdom. It is an organisation devoted to preventing and resolving employment disputes.

Accessibility audit

An audit of either your organisation's accessibility (e.g. headquarters accessibility for wheelchair users) or its online products and services (e.g. ability for a visually impaired member to access your website or online members' area via a screen reader). Inaccessible offerings may put a membership organisation or professional association at risk of legal action.

Accountability

In ethics and governance, accountability is answerability, blameworthiness, liability, and the expectation of account-giving. As an aspect of governance, it has been central to discussions related to problems in the public sector, non-profit and private sector corporate worlds. In leadership roles, accountability is the acknowledgement and assumption of responsibility for actions, products, decisions and policies, including administration, governance and implementation within the scope of the role and encompassing the obligation to report, explain and be answerable for resulting consequences.

Accountable – see also RASCI definitions

The person to whom "R - responsible" is Accountable and is the authority who has final approval.

Accounting – see also Budgeting

The systematic and comprehensive recording of financial transactions of a business, as well as the process of summarising, analysing and reporting these transactions.

Accreditation

A voluntary method of quality assurance which is both a status and a process, e.g. Investors in People. As a status, accreditation provides public notification that an institution, programme or individual meets standards of quality set by an accrediting agency. As a process, accreditation reflects the fact that in achieving recognition by the accrediting agency, the programme, institution or individual is committed to external review in seeking not only to meet standards but to continuously seek ways in which to enhance the quality of education, training or services provided. See also Academic accreditation.

Accrual / Accrued cost

The cost of work that has been done but for which payment is not yet due.

Action plan

An action plan is a document that lists what steps must be taken in order to achieve a specific goal or goals. Its purpose is to clarify what resources are required to reach the goal and formulate a time line for when specific tasks need to be completed.

Actual cost

The actual money spent in performing an activity so far. The total actual cost may include elements of Accruals (see entry) or Committed costs (see entry).

Acquisition – see also Merger

Taking possession of an asset by purchase, ranging from materials and equipment to buildings or part or all of another organisation in order to fulfil strategic intent.

Ad hoc co-operation

An unplanned, improvised or impromptu co-operation within or between individuals or organisations.

Ad hoc meeting

An unplanned, improvised or impromptu meeting convened when a specific need arises.

Advisory board / group / committee

A group convened to provide direction (operational and/or strategic) on a particular topic, activity or theme. Such groups may form part of the regular structure of the organisation or may be created for a particular purpose or project and disbanded when the work is complete.

Advocacy – see also Lobbying

A process of political activity by an individual or group which aims to influence policy and resource allocation decisions. Advocacy by a person or organisation can take many forms including media campaigns, public speaking, commissioning and publishing research. An organisation's own members can be their most effective advocates.

Affiliate marketing

Third party advertising of membership and/or related benefits usually in return for an agreed fee (either percentage or fixed).

Affiliate member

Affiliate membership is usually offered to individuals or organisations that do not meet or have not yet met the criteria for higher levels of membership. From a governance perspective this grade of membership is usually non-voting and professional bodies granting this grade of membership will not ordinarily include the use of Post-nominals (letters after the member's name) (see entry). It can also be used to include those interested in the organisation's activities.

Affiliate programme

From a membership organisation or professional association perspective this type of programme or scheme enables individuals or organisations to be affiliated with an organisation. In many cases this type of scheme enables affiliation of organisations or individuals who may not meet specific membership criteria, e.g. complementary professions or suppliers, but who nonetheless express an ongoing interest.

Affinity membership scheme – see also Value added scheme

A growing number of membership organisations and associations are providing members with access to schemes which provide access to preferential offers and discounts and provide the organisation with an opportunity to demonstrate added or enhanced membership value (directly contributing to the organisation's Member value proposition – see entry). Schemes can either be created (i.e. offers and discounts negotiated with providers within a specific trade, profession or specialism which the organisation represents) or procured via third party organisations. The former is likely to generate direct streams of income whilst the latter will mostly be paid-for by the organisation.

Affinity partners / Affinity marketing

A concept that consists of a partnership, usually financial, between a commercial company and an organisation where the company is asked to provide a product or service to the organisation's members. This increases brand loyalty for both company and organisation as well as the products themselves and heightens market awareness of both.

Agenda

A list of items or activities to be discussed at a formal meeting listed in the order in which they are to be addressed.

Agile working

Agile working practices make clear that work is an activity not a place and will incorporate elements of time and place flexibility but also involve doing work differently, focusing on performance and outcomes. It is usually transformational.

AGM - see Annual general meeting

Agreements

Agreements can take many forms at varying levels of importance, however formal agreements will usually be agreed via consensus (e.g. committee) and will be formalised via a formal document (e.g. Minutes or Agreement document).

Alliance(s) – see also Coalitions

Most formal alliances are forged between organisations with a shared common interest or ideal. A likely objective would be that combined effort will generate optimal results as, for example, when two organisations conduct similar work. A working example would be a group of medical associations forging an alliance to lobby government on a particular health concern with the shared interest of improving public health.

Alumni membership scheme

An alumnus (male) or alumna (female) is a graduate of a school, college or university. A large number of these institutions run Alumni schemes that enable the organisation to continue a direct relationship with graduates. Opportunities or benefits for alumni might include a journal, events, discounts and volunteering opportunities, as well as opportunities to donate. Many universities encourage Alumni to donate money towards library books or Benevolent funds (see entry).

Amortisation

The gradual elimination of a liability, such as a loan, in regular payments over a specified period of time. Such payments must be sufficient to cover both principal and interest. Also the spreading out of capital expenses for intangible assets over a specific period of time - usually over the asset's useful life - for accounting and tax purposes. Similar to Depreciation (see entry) which is used for tangible assets and to depletion which is used for natural resources.

Analytics – see also Reporting and analytics

Analytics is the discovery and communication of meaningful patterns in data. Key examples of the usage of this word within the membership and association sector include web analytics and membership survey analytics.

Annual conference

Most membership organisations and professional associations hold an annual conference for members. Likely content may include lectures, seminars, fringe sessions, a trade exhibition, social functions and poster competitions.

Annual general meeting (AGM)

A meeting that happens once every year in which a company or other organisation presents the annual report, discusses the past year's activities and financial results and elects new officers. See also Extraordinary general meeting (EGM).

Annual hump

This term is used to describe a marked increase in the number of joiners, renewers or lapsed members at a particular time of year. This may happen for a number of reasons, e.g. start of the financial or membership year. Sometimes known as the peak.

Annual renewals – see also Fixed renewals

This membership scheme model requires all members to renew on a set date or within a specific time period, usually on an annual basis. This is probably one of the oldest paid-for membership scheme models in existence and is often referred to as fixed renewal.

Annual report

A formal document, published annually, that is likely to contain the membership organisation or association's published set of accounts (including profit and loss statement, balance sheet, cash flow statement, total recognised gains and losses and notes to the accounts). The document may include a strategy statement from the Chief Executive or Chair for the period (highlighting key achievements and events) and the most recent auditor's report. In the United Kingdom this document must be submitted to the Charity Commission (see entry) which is the national charity regulator.

Annual return

In the United Kingdom it is the responsibility of the Company secretary to submit this document every year to Companies House where the company is registered. It includes information on the type of company, registered address, names of directors, etc, and is distinct from the company's annual accounts and tax return.

Annual review

A full review of an organisation's products, services, and activities in the previous year to assess which elements of the organisation are to be continued, refreshed or removed. This activity is usually part of an ongoing Business planning cycle – see entry.

Appeals process / Appeals panel - see also Complaints procedure

A process or panel put in place to enable individuals or organisations to appeal against decisions made. Many membership organisations and professional associations have panels that review the decision made when a membership upgrade application is declined. Other examples can include examination results, certification processes and disciplinary issues.

Application process

The process which enables individuals or organisations to join a membership organisation or association. Traditionally application processes were administered in hardcopy, however most organisations have moved to enabling applications online.

Appraisal process - see also Performance appraisal, Performance review, Performance evaluation

A method by which the job performance of an employee is evaluated. Performance appraisals are an important part of Career development (see entry) and usually consist of regular reviews of employee performance within organisations.

Apps

A mobile application (or mobile app) is a software application designed to run on smart phones, tablets and other mobile devices. Some apps are free, while others must be purchased.

Arbitration – see also Mediation

Arbitration is a well-established and widely used means to end disputes. It provides both parties with a choice other than litigation and usually takes place out of court. The two sides select an impartial third party, known as an arbitrator, agree in advance to comply with the arbitrator's decision and then participate in a hearing at which both sides can present evidence and testimony. The arbitrator's decision is usually final and courts rarely re-examine it.

Archive

An archive is an accumulation of historical records, or the physical place where they are located. Archives contain primary source documents that have accumulated over the course of an individual or organisation's lifetime, and are kept to show the function or history of that person or organisation. There are a range of legal and financial obligations which govern the need for retention of specific documents for specific periods of time. Professional archivists and historians generally understand archives to be records that have been naturally and necessarily generated as a product of regular legal, commercial, administrative or social activities.

Asset

A useful or valuable thing, quality or person, e.g. organisational ability is a personal asset.

Assets

The entire property of all kinds belonging to a trading association or membership organisation. Items of ownership convertible into cash; total resources of a person or business, as cash, notes and accounts receivable, securities, inventories, goodwill, fixtures, machinery, or real estate (as opposed to Liabilities – see entry).

Associate member

Although definitions of specific membership grades vary between organisations, an associate member is likely to be defined as a person who is a member but has only partial rights and privileges or subordinate status. Many professional bodies grant associate membership to individuals who are in training. Typically this grade of membership does not carry Post-nominals (letters after your name) (see entry) and from a governance perspective is non-voting.

Association

A legal form or structure of governance. The unincorporated association is a very common, relatively informal structure for voluntary and community organisations of all types. They are membership-based and encourage an active membership as an appropriate method of promoting participation. The word association may be used in a wider context to describe an organisational type which may, in fact be a limited company and not structured as an association.

Association management company (AMC)

An external, outsourced company employed to conduct association related activity ranging from specific activities to full service. Examples of outsourced activity may include membership subscription renewal activity, meeting administration, ad-hoc mailings and event or conference registration.

Assumptions

Accepting and acting as if certain facts are correct without checking if they are true or looking for proof. In projects, assumptions are statements that will be taken for granted as fact and upon which the project business case will be justified. Making unfounded assumptions can lead to poor decision making and service delivery.

Asynchronous learning – see also eLearning and Synchronous learning

The term describes a student-centred teaching method that uses online learning resources to facilitate information sharing outside the constraints of time and place among a network of people.

Attributes

Defined as characteristics, qualities or properties. Attributes fall into several categories: mental, physical and emotional.

Attrition rate – see also Churn rate

Sometimes called Churn rate. In its broadest sense, it is a measure of the number of individuals or items moving out of a collective or organisation over a specific period of time. It can also be used to measure marketing return on investment.

Audit / Auditor / Audit committee

A systematic evaluation of how finances are being managed against a predetermined set of criteria. An audit committee will be a sub-set of the main board. The auditor's role is to carefully check the accuracy of the organisation's business records and is frequently independent of the organisation.

Automated emails

These are emails which can be triggered after a particular action or event, e.g. an automated welcome email when someone has successfully joined or an automated email receipt when an online purchase is made.

Awarding body

An awarding body (previously known as an examination or exam body) is an organisation empowered to 'make awards', or 'award qualifications'. This function should not be confused with similar functions such as award recognition or licence to practice, which normally resides with certain professional organisations. An awarding body does not always provide courses that lead to a qualification. The can often provide an approval process for independent training providers who, if they meet the criteria, are able to award qualifications that are accredited by that awarding body. Any qualification from an awarding body is clearly identified as being at one of nine levels which have approximate equivalences with academic qualifications.

B

B2B

Also known as 'B to B' or 'Business to Business'. A type of commercial transaction that exists between businesses, such as those involving a manufacturer and wholesaler, or a wholesaler and a retailer. Business to business refers to business that is conducted between companies, rather than between a company and individual consumers.

B2C

Also known as 'Business to Consumer'. Business or transactions conducted directly between a company and consumers who are the end-users of its products or services.

B2G

Also known as 'Business to Government'. Professional affairs conducted between companies and national, regional or municipal governing bodies. Business to government typically encompasses the determination and evaluation of government agency needs, the creation and submission of proposals and the completion of the contracted work.

Baby boomers – see also Generational differences

A person who was born during the post-World War II baby boom between the years 1946 and 1964. The term "baby boomer" is also used in a cultural context and is associated with a rejection or redefinition of traditional values. Regarded as the most physically fit generation up to that date and amongst the first to grow up genuinely expecting the world to improve over time.

Balance sheet

A statement of the assets, liabilities, and capital of a business or other organisation at a particular point in time, detailing the balance of income and expenditure over the preceding period.

Balanced scorecard – see also Dashboards

A strategic planning and management system that is used extensively in business and industry, government, and non-profit organisations worldwide to align business activities to the vision and strategy of the organisation, improve internal and external communications, and monitor organisation performance against strategic goals. It adds strategic non-financial performance measures to traditional financial metrics to give managers and executives a more 'balanced' view of organisational performance. Often utilising RAG reports (see entry).

Ballot or Ballot paper – see also Elections

Ballots are used to cast votes (usually by members) in an election. Each voter is normally entitled to one ballot and they are not usually shared. Versions of acceptable ballot arrangements range from a piece of paper or pre-printed/merged form through to online voting, depending on the organisation and the context. Ballots usually take place as part of or in conjunction with either a committee meeting, board meeting or Annual general meeting (AGM) or Extraordinary general meeting (EGM). Votes are usually cast anonymously and placed in a ballot box and, when counted, it is good practice to have an independent monitor to ensure the count process is accurate, conducted professionally and according to the requirements of the Memorandum and Articles of Association (see entry).

Baseline

A baseline is a measure of anything that may change, before it is changed.

Belbin's team roles

Belbin team roles describe and measure behaviour, not personality, and so can be defined as: A tendency to behave, contribute and interrelate with others in a particular way. The team roles that Meredith Belbin identified are today used widely in thousands of organisations all over the world.

Beliefs
Assumptions and convictions that a person holds to be true regarding people, concepts or things.

Benchmarking
The process of comparing one's business processes and performance metrics to industry bests, best practices from other industries or against standards. Areas typically measured are products, quality, time, cost and procedures.

Benchmark measures
A set of measurements (metrics) used to establish goals for performance improvements. These are often derived from other organisations thought to display best practice performance.

Benefits
All projects and programmes must deliver some form of benefit to the host organisation as a result of investing time and other resources otherwise there is no point in undertaking the work.

Benefit packages – see also Member benefits
Various additional compensations provided to members in addition to their normal membership benefits.

Benevolent fund - see also Grant giving
A fund of money set aside to give aid or support to members who find themselves in difficult financial circumstances, generally to relieve poverty.

Best practice - see also Industry standard and Good practice
Recognised and/or determined practices and processes that are known to deliver positive or optimal results. A method or technique that has consistently shown results superior to those achieved with other means, and that is used as a benchmark. Best practice can evolve to become better as improvements are discovered. Used to describe the process of developing and following a standard way of doing things that multiple

organisations can use. Best practices are used to maintain quality as an alternative to mandatory legislated standards and can be based on self-assessment or benchmarking. A feature of accredited management standards such as ISO 9000 (Quality management) and ISO 14001 (Environmental management).

Bid candy

This is the term used when bidding organisations speak with affiliate or supply chain companies or organisations and name them as being ready, willing and able to help them achieve their goals in order to make their bid or tender more attractive. They don't actually work with them when the contract is won.

Big data

The term for a collection of data or data sets (ordinarily about members and/or related activity) that is large and complex (sometimes difficult) to process using database management tools or more traditional data processing applications.

Blank sheet exercise

Starting any discussion or planning event without any pre-conceived ideas of what the outcome should look like.

Blended learning – see also eLearning and Online learning

An education programme which incorporates more than one medium or platform of training or learning delivery. There is normally an assumption that this will include some elements of eLearning with some element of student control over time, place, path, and/or pace.

Blog / Blogging

A discussion or informational site published on the internet and consisting of discrete entries (posts) typically displayed in reverse chronological order (the most recent post appears first). They are usually the work of a single individual (e.g. President, Chair or Chief Executive), occasionally of a small group, and often covering a single subject or topic area.

BME – Black and minority ethnic

BME is an acronym which stands for Black and Minority Ethnic and is most often used to refer to groups or policies that affect people from non-white-UK ethnic backgrounds.

Board

The body that is legally responsible and accountable for governing and controlling the organisation, sometimes called council, management committee, board of directors, board of trustees, executive or governing body, etc.

Board of directors – see also Executive committee

Group of directors appointed to act on behalf of, and within the powers granted to them by, the board of directors. Typically in a membership organisation or professional association it consists of a chairperson, vice-chairperson, secretary and treasurer.

Board member – see also Trustee board

A board member is an elected or appointed member of the board of directors that oversees the activities of an association or membership organisation. Other variations of this term may include trustee board member or trustee. They are legally accountable for the organisation's work and are usually unpaid although legitimate travel or subsistence expenses are often provided.

Body of knowledge

The term refers to a definition of the current agreed extent or best practice in a particular profession.

Bounced email

When an email message cannot be delivered to an email address, it's called a bounce and a "return to sender" message is sent from the recipient's mail server to explain why. A soft bounce is a temporary delivery failure, i.e. the email address was recognised but the message bounced back undelivered instead of reaching the recipient's inbox. A hard bounce is a permanent delivery failure, i.e. the recipient's email address is invalid or no longer in use. The bounce rate (considered healthy at 2-3%) is the number of bounced emails divided by the total number of recipients the campaign was sent to. Bounce rates are directly related to the quality of the subscriber list. High bounce rates indicate that there may be problems with the way the list was grown, or how it is being managed.

Brainstorming

A group or individual creativity technique by which efforts are made to find a conclusion for a specific problem by gathering a list of ideas spontaneously contributed by its member(s). Each person is asked to think creatively and contribute as many ideas as possible which are then discussed as a group. Brainstorming was claimed to be more effective than individuals working alone in generating ideas, although more recent research has questioned this conclusion. Today, the term is used as a catch all for group ideation sessions or envisioning activities. The politically correct term Thought shower is now also being used to describe these types of activities.

Branch network - see also Chapters, Local member networks and Regional structure

Member networks can be structured into geographical branches (e.g. London) and sections (e.g. South West London). Typically branches will have a formalised structure and may be governed by a committee comprising a Chair, Treasurer and Secretary. Branches are either administered by volunteer members, funded centrally or self-funded. May include national branches of international organisations.

Branch structure – see also Branch network

The national or international structure of branches affiliated to or part of the membership.

Brand

A name, term, sign, symbol, Logo or design, or a combination of them intended to identify the goods and services of a business or organisation and to differentiate them from those of other sellers of potentially similar items.

Brand image / Identity

The impression and opinion that the public has of a product, person or organisation. Safeguarding and enhancing an organisation's public identity is an important part of its marketing activities.

Brand management

The application of marketing techniques to a specific product, product line, brand, service or organisation. A way to position in the market and get your prospects to see your product or service as the only one that provides a solution to their problem.

Budgeting - see also Accounting and Financial strategy

A budget is a quantitative statement of resources (usually monetary) required to achieve a particular objective.

Business case

A business case is essential for all major activities, projects and programmes. It justifies the existence of the activity by defining what Benefits (see entry) are to be achieved and the estimated cost. The business case must also explain why the benefits are worth the estimated expenditure and will usually contain the results of one or more forms of investment appraisal and/or the anticipated effects of the scenario in which nothing is done.

Business change – see also Change management

An approach to transitioning individuals, teams and organisations to a desired future state, often via a process of Project management (see entry).

Business continuity planning (BCP) – see also Risk management

A business continuity plan details how an organisation would continue operations if a place of business (e.g. an office, work site or data centre) is affected by adverse physical conditions, such as a storm, fire or crime. Such a plan typically explains how the business would recover its operations or move operations to another location. For example, if a fire destroys an office building or data centre, the people and operations would relocate to an alternate site. The plan should include recovering from different levels of disaster which would range from short term, localised disasters to the permanent loss of a building or all staff.

Business intelligence

A data analysis process aimed at boosting business performance by helping corporate executives and other end users make more informed decisions. It encompasses a variety of tools, applications and methodologies that enable organisations to collect data from internal systems and external sources, prepare it for analysis, develop and run queries against the data, and create reports, dashboards, and data visualisations to make the analytical results available to decision makers as well as operational workers.

Buy-in

Acceptance of and willingness to actively support and participate in something, e.g. a proposed new plan or policy.

By-Laws (also Byelaws)

A set of rules and regulations enacted by an association or membership body to regulate itself internally and provide a framework for its operation, activities and management. By-laws specify the qualifications, rights and liabilities of membership as well as the powers, duties and grounds for the dissolution of the organisation. They should not be confused with the Memorandum and Articles of Association (see entry) and are, in effect, a contract among members and must be formally adopted and/or amended.

C

Campaign

A programme of work which details an organised and active route towards a specified goal.

Campaign strategies

Strategies linked to current and/or proposed future marketing or membership campaign activity.

Canvassing opinion

The process of conversing with members or stakeholders to establish a view of the range of opinion on a particular topic or issue, potentially requesting votes as well as opinions.

Capacity

The capability of a worker, system or organisation to produce output per time period. It can be classified as budgeted, dedicated, demonstrated, productive, protective, rated, safety or theoretical.

Capital budgeting

Also known as investment appraisal. The process in which a business determines whether projects such as investing in a new long-term venture are worth pursuing. Often a prospective project's lifetime cash inflows and outflows are assessed in order to determine whether the returns generated meet a sufficient target benchmark.

Career development

The lifelong process of managing and developing work-related knowledge, experience and competence in order to progress. For those working within specific professions these elements will be detailed in sector relevant competence frameworks.

Career stage

Professional associations and membership organisations offer career-stage specific support. Most take a cradle to grave approach and many segment audiences via career stage due to varying demands and requirements.

Case studies (Case report)

A descriptive, exploratory or explanatory analysis of a person, group or event. An explanatory case study is used to explore causation in order to find or develop underlying principles.

Cash flow

The movement of money into or out of a business, project, or financial product, usually measured during a specified, limited period of time. This can be impacted directly by increases and decreases in new member recruitment, existing member retention and business/membership development activities.

Cash flow forecast

A cash flow forecast indicates the likely future movement of cash in and out of the business. It's an estimate of the amount of money expected to flow in (receipts) and out (payments) of the business and includes all projected income and expenses. A forecast usually covers the next 12 months but it can also cover a short-term period such as a week or month.

CBE – see also Computer based examinations

Students, studying members and trainees progress and achieve qualifications by demonstrating their competence, which means they prove that they have mastered the knowledge and skills required for a particular course. Competence-based education allows students to study and learn at their own pace and is particularly ideal for those without formal higher qualifications. The fundamental premise of competence-based education is that what students should know and be able to do is clearly defined and they graduate when they have demonstrated their competence.

Certification – see also Qualification

Confirmation of knowledge, skill or competence within a

particular area that is often provided via external review, assessment, audit or review. See also Accreditation.

Certification body

A body ordinarily responsible for administering, managing or developing the process and criteria for certification.

Certification board or committee

A group ordinarily responsible for the governance, leadership, criteria and development of the certification process it oversees.

Chair of the board

May also be known as chairman or chairperson.   The highest officer or member of the board. This person is typically elected by the board and/or voting members. The relationship between the Chair and the Chief Executive Officer is of paramount importance in the success of the organisation.

Chamber of commerce

A chamber of commerce represents organisations in all sectors operating within a particular geographical area. Any representational work is confined to local issues. Generic training and promotion are among the functions of local chambers.

Change management – see also Business change and Organisational change

An approach to transitioning individuals, teams and organisations to a desired future state, often via a process of Project management (see entry).

Chapters – see also Branch network and Regional structure

A term used for particular and often structured regional groups or branches. These are often governed by local committees comprising a Chair (often elected to a national board or council), Secretary and Treasurer. Many organisations provide limited funding (based on a per capita or member basis) and more advanced organisations require regular reporting back to HQ.

Activity may include local conferences, social events and local mentoring schemes.

Character

The sum total of an individual's personality Traits and the link between a person's values and behaviour. Organisations are also said to exhibit character for the same reasons.

Charitable incorporated organisation (CIO)

A charitable incorporated organisation is a new legal form of governance for a charity. It is designed to remove the requirement for organisations to have dual registration with both Companies House and the Charity Commission. The organisation will be singly registered with the Charity Commission and will ease the burden of regulation.

Charitable objects – see also Objects

The terms used to describe and identify the goals, aims and purpose for which the charity or non-profit organisation has been set up.

Charitable purpose

In order for an organisation to demonstrate charitable purpose it must: 1 - Fall within one of the four charitable purposes set out in Section 5(1) of the Charities Act; 2 - Provide a Public benefit, and 3 - Not be aimed at creating private financial profit.

Charitable status

A charity is neither a legal form nor a type of organisation but a separate legal status that may apply to some organisations. In order to be a charity an organisation must: 1 – exist for purposes that the law recognises as exclusively charitable; and 2 – exist for the Public benefit.

Charitable trust

A form of trust established for charitable purposes.

Charities Act

The Charities Act 2011 is a UK Act of Parliament which consolidated the bulk of the previous Charities Act 2006, outstanding provisions of the Charities Act 1993, and various other enactments. The Charities Act 2006 provided a new statutory definition of charity, based on a list of headings of charitable purposes, and re-emphasised the importance of Public benefit. The Act also gave the Charity Commission a new objective of promoting awareness and understanding of the public benefit requirement, and of issuing guidance on public benefit.

Charity

A non-profit organisation set up to provide philanthropic or social well-being goals, often with educational or other activities serving the Public interest or common good.

Charity Commission

The Commission is the regulator for charities in England and Wales. It is a non-Ministerial Government Department, part of the Civil Service. The Commission is completely independent of Ministerial influence and also independent from the sector it regulates. It has a number of quasi-judicial functions where it uses powers similar to those of the High Court.

Chartered Institute - see also Royal Charter and Privy Council

A professional body incorporated under or with Royal Charter (a formal document issued by a monarch as letters patent, granting a right or power to an individual or a body corporate).

Chartered member/professional

A chartered professional is a person who has gained a level of competence in a particular field of work and, in recognition, has been awarded a formal credential by an organisation to which they belong. It is considered a status of professional competence and chartered status is awarded mainly by professional bodies. Common in Britain and in the Commonwealth, it has been adopted by organisations around the world.

Chartered status originates from and may normally only be awarded by Institutions that have been incorporated under Royal Charter (see entry) by the British Monarch, hence its prevalent use in the UK and Commonwealth countries. However, such is the prestige and credibility of a chartered designation that some non-UK organisations have taken to issuing chartered designations without Royal or Parliamentary approval.

Chatham House Rule

The Royal Institute of International Affairs is based at Chatham House in London and is often known by that name. The Chatham House Rule is invoked at meetings to encourage free discussions. It states that:
"When a meeting, or part thereof, is held under the Chatham House Rule, participants are free to use the information received, but neither the identity nor the affiliation of the speaker(s), nor that of any other participant, may be revealed." Many security conferences and organisations use the Chatham House Rule for their meetings.

Checklists

A structured way to ensure core or peripheral tasks are completed in order to achieve a desired outcome, e.g. membership application checklist. This may feature in the joining or renewal literature or forms to ensure all required documentation is in place. This can help in avoiding the need for follow-up or extra membership administration work, thereby making savings in time, resources and budget.

Chief Executive Officer (CEO) – see also Secretary General and General Manager

Most associations and membership organisations have a CEO (or equivalent) in place who is the highest ranking paid management officer in the organisation with responsibility for human, financial and technical operations, as well as delivery

of the organisation's strategy. Typically the CEO is accountable
to the Board of Directors (or Board of Trustees). Alternative job
titles may include Chief Executive or Director General. In some
organisations the role may be carried out by the President if
there is no employed member of staff at this level.

Chief Information Officer (CIO)
Chief Information Officer, sometimes known as the Information
Technology (IT) director, is a job title commonly given to the
most senior executive in an organisation responsible for the
information technology and computer systems that support the
organisation's goals.

Churn rate – see also Attrition rate

CIO – see Charitable incorporated organisation

Civil Society
Society considered as a community of citizens linked by
common interests and collective activity.

Click through rate – see also E-newsletters and Open rate
A way of measuring the success of an online campaign via the
click-through rate (the number of clicks a URL receives within
either an electronic publication or campaign). Typically the
rate is higher for membership organisations and professional
associations than commercial suppliers and can be used as one
of a number of indicators (including Open Rate) to evaluate
engagement or campaign success.

Climate (internal to an organisation) – see also Employee engagement
The short-term phenomenon created by the current mix of
junior and senior managers. Organisational climate relates
to the perception of people about the organisation and its
leaders, directly attributed to the leadership and management
style of the leaders, based on the skills, knowledge, attitude
and priorities of the leaders. The personality and behaviour of
the leaders creates a climate that influences everyone in the

organisation.

CMS (Content management system)

A content management system (CMS) is a computer programme that allows publishing, editing and modifying of content as well as maintenance from a central interface. Such systems of content management provide procedures to manage workflow in a collaborative environment. These procedures can be manual steps or an automated cascade. CMSs have been available since the late 1990s. They are often used to run corporate and marketing websites containing blogs, news and shopping. CMSs typically aim to avoid the need for hard coding but may support it for specific elements or entire pages.

Coaching – see also Mentoring and Peer support

Coaching and mentoring are development techniques based on the use of one-to-one discussions to enhance an individual's skills, knowledge or work performance in order to achieve their full potential. It is possible to draw distinctions between coaching and mentoring although in practice the two terms are often used interchangeably. Coaching targets high performance and improvement at work and usually focuses on specific skills and goals, although it may also have an impact on an individual's personal attributes (such as social interaction or confidence). The process typically lasts for a relatively short period.

Coalitions – see also Alliances

A temporary alliance between two or more organisations for combined action. Typically used by associations or membership organisations for government lobbying and/or national or wide scale public sector awareness campaigning.

Co-branding

Associates a single product or service with more than one brand name.

Coded feedback – see also Member feedback

A structured method for analysing feedback results (sometimes unstructured) from research findings, e.g. the responses from an annual membership survey. Open question may pick up particular themes that can be coded into a particular topic such as a requirement for more lobbying activity.

Code of conduct / Code of professional conduct

A set of rules outlining the responsibilities of or proper practices for an individual, profession or organisation.

Code of ethics

Adopted by organisations to assist members in understanding the difference between right and wrong and in applying that understanding to their decisions. An ethical code generally implies documents at three levels: codes of business ethics, codes of conduct for employees, and codes of professional practice for members.

Code of practice

Written guidelines issued by an official body or a professional association to its members to help them comply with the ethical standards required by that organisation or by the profession it represents.

Colour type personality theory

A personality profiling tool, created by Dr Taylor Hartman. The main idea behind the profiling is that all people possess one of four driving "core motives" which divides personalities into four colours: Red (motivated by power), Blue (motivated by intimacy), White (motivated by peace), and Yellow (motivated by fun).

Commercial awareness

A general knowledge and understanding of business, business experience and/or understanding a particular industry or industries.

Commercial services

Products or services provided by a membership organisation or association and/or subsidiaries that are either commercial in nature or are managed or administered to make a profit or surplus.

Commissioning

The authority to undertake or perform certain duties or functions, usually defined as the process of ensuring that services are provided effectively and that they meet the needs of the relevant population.

Committed costs

Costs which an activity or project is contractually obliged to pay, regardless of whether the product or service has actually been delivered or invoiced.

Committee – see also Panel

A deliberative assembly of members/stakeholders that ordinarily meets on a regular basis and remains the subordinate to a more senior authority (e.g. the Board of Trustees or Council). They may hold delegated responsibility from the main Board.

Communications channels

Communication channels are the means through which people in any organisation communicate with each other and with their members and other stakeholders. Different channels are used to complete various tasks as using an inappropriate channel for a task or interaction can lead to negative or unforeseen consequences. Complex messages require richer channels of communication that facilitate interaction in order to ensure clarity. Differing channels include face-to-face, written, mobile, electronic and broadcast media.

Communications – internal

The communication between stakeholders (e.g. staff, officers, committee members) within a professional association or membership organisation.

Communications – external

The communication to individuals external to a professional association or membership organisation (e.g. members, general public).

Communications plan

A communications plan provides a structured overview of the content to be communicated, the audience to be communicated to, the communications vehicles to be used, and the timing(s) of the communications.

Communications strategy/schedule

A single, coherent narrative that describes a communications solution designed to reinforce positive aspects of the organisation and its services or to a deal with a problem or bundle of problems an association or membership organisation and/or its members, stakeholders or the general public currently faces. Working at a strategic level, it sets out the nature of the problem or challenge, the key considerations in addressing it, the choices that have been made, the key drivers of those decisions, the resources required, the stages to go through and the evaluation criteria. It differs from a communications plan as it considers the wider context, refers to the longer term and avoids operational and tactical detail.

Community interest company (CIC)

A new legal form of governance structure introduced by the United Kingdom government in 2005 under the Companies (Audit, Investigations and Community Enterprise) Act 2004, designed for social enterprises that want to use their profits and assets for the public good. CICs are intended to be easy to set up, with all the flexibility and certainty of the company form, but with some special features to ensure they are working for the benefit of the community. They are regulated by the CIC Regulator.

Community of practice (CoP)

A group of people who share a craft or profession. The group may evolve naturally over time due to members' common interest in a particular domain or area, or it can be created specifically with the goal of gaining knowledge related to a specific field. Through a process of sharing information and experiences the group members learn from each other and develop personally and professionally. CoPs can exist online, such as within discussion boards and newsgroups, or in real life.

Companies House

Companies House is the United Kingdom's registrar of companies and is an executive agency and trading fund of Her Majesty's Government. It falls under the remit of the Department for Business, Innovation and Skills (BIS) and is also a member of the Public Data Group. All forms of companies are incorporated and registered with Companies House and file specific details as required by the current Companies Act 2006. All registered limited companies, including subsidiary, small and inactive companies, must file annual financial statements in addition to annual company returns, which are all public records. Only some registered unlimited companies are exempt from this requirement.

Company limited by guarantee

In UK and Irish company law, a private company limited by guarantee is an alternative type of corporation used primarily for non-profit organisations that require legal personality. A company limited by guarantee does not usually have a share capital or shareholders, but instead has members who act as guarantors.

Company limited by shares

A private company limited by shares, usually called a private limited company (Ltd.) (though this can theoretically also refer to a private company limited by guarantee), is a type of company incorporated under the laws of England, Wales and Scotland, that of certain Commonwealth countries and the

Republic of Ireland. It has shareholders with limited liability and its shares may not be offered to the general public, unlike those of a public limited company (plc).

Company Secretary – see also Secretary

Many professional associations and membership organisations employ a company secretary who oversees a range of governance and legal issues, e.g. ensuring that company accounts are submitted on time.

Competence / Competency – see also Core competences

The ability of an individual to do something successfully, effectively or efficiently, often measured against a prescribed standard.

Competence based exams – see CBE

Competence framework

A structured framework that codifies or outlines the key competencies required in order to effectively conduct a particular activity or role. A set of defined abilities that provide a structured guide enabling the identification, evaluation and development of required behaviours in individuals or in professions.

Competition

The effort of two or more parties acting independently to secure the business of a third party by offering the most favourable terms. In the association and membership organisation sector competition can exist between organisations within various industries.

Complaints procedure - see also Appeals Process

Many membership organisations or professional associations have formalised processes and procedures in order to deal consistently and effectively with complaints. These can relate to member v member, member v organisation, organisation v organisation, member of the public v member.

Components
>Parts or elements of which anything is made up or into which it may be resolved.

Computer based examinations - see CBE

Confederation
>An umbrella organisation consisting of representatives from different membership organisations, associations and/or stakeholder organisations, each governing itself but also working together in an alliance for business or political reasons.

Conflict of interest
>Any business activity, either personal or company related, that has the capacity to interfere with the organisation's goals. Ordinarily conflicts of interest occur when an individual or organisation participating in membership organisation or association business (e.g. committee members) have a conflict of self-interest (linked directly to themselves or people/organisations they are involved or associated with). Requiring all officers to complete a formal 'Conflict of Interest' form can enable membership organisations and associations to address this issue by ensuring that all such relationships are declared and visible.

Consensus building
>Working towards the adoption of a general agreement on a particular subject or topic, e.g. by members, between organisations and/or with government.

Constant Professional Engagement (CPE)
>This term addresses the idea that CPD is now evolving, mainly due to the changes in the way professionals utilise social media and interpersonal networking. The effect of engaging all the time with other professionals will add ideas and enhance learning, providing enhancements to each individual's body of knowledge. Membership organisations and associations will need to understand and acknowledge the effect this has on

enhancing skills both for members and staff.

Constitution – see also MemArts and Memorandum and Articles of
Association
A set of fundamental principles or established precedents
according to which a professional association or membership
organisation is governed.

Constraint
Any element or factor that prevents a person, a group of people
or an organisation from reaching a higher level of agreement or
performance with respect to a specific goal.

Constructive dismissal
In employment law, constructive dismissal (also called
constructive discharge) occurs when employees resign because
their employer's behaviour has become so intolerable or made
life so difficult that the employee has no choice but to resign.
Since such a resignation will not be truly voluntary, it is in effect
a termination. In general, constructive dismissal leads to the
employee's obligations ending and the employee acquiring the
right to make claims against the employer.

Consultant
An external professional who provides expert advice in a
particular area. For professional associations and membership
organisations these individuals might provide advice on
governance, strategic development, delivery and planning,
creation of professional frameworks, membership marketing
strategy.

Consultation with membership
Activity associated with enabling members or stakeholders
to input directly into proposed changes or development of a
membership organisation or professional association activity,
initiative or standpoint.

Consulted – see also RASCI definitions
> A person who provides information and/or expertise necessary to complete the work.

Contact
> This term ordinarily refers to the main point of contact linked to a member record. Therefore this is the person who receives correspondence, emails and renewal subscription literature.

Content management
> Content management has increased significantly in recent years due to the significant content published online (see Content Management System/CMS) and offline (see Archive).

Contingency
> Plans or arrangements made in case a particular risk situation should arise.

Contract of employment
> A formal agreement between an employer and employee about the terms and conditions of employment and is the basis of the employment relationship.

Continuing educational training (CET) – see also Continuing professional development
> This term is used within a number of industries in place of continuing professional development, e.g. optometry, where the requirements for an individual's development are more formalised.

Continuing professional development (CPD) - see also CPD schemes and Online CPD
> Continuing professional development (CPD) is the means by which individuals maintain their knowledge and skills, related to their professional lives, through professional learning and development over the full length of their career.

Conversion

Conversion refers to desired transactions of different types. Membership conversion identifies the transition from either non-member to member or from one category of membership to another, e.g. student member to full member or member to fellow. Many organisations use the annual number of member conversions (or percentage) as an annual membership related target or key performance indicator.

Conversion can also refer to converting visitors to delegates either relative to the website or to events.

Copyright - see also Intellectual property rights

The exclusive and assignable legal right given to the originator (e.g. individual, association or membership organisation) for a fixed number of years to print or publish content online and/ or offline. Within organisations, copyright is rarely held by the individual who compiled the content but is held instead by the employing organisation. A clause detailing this right usually forms part of the contract of employment.

Core competences – see also Competence

A specific set of attributes that a professional association or membership organisation believes are central to the way the organisation and/or its members work. Often defined as fundamental knowledge, ability or expertise in a specific subject area or skill set. A core competence can take various forms, including technical/subject matter know-how, a reliable process and/or relationship building with customers and suppliers.

Core values

Core values are the fundamental beliefs of the professional association or membership organisation and members normally join the organisation to demonstrate this shared belief. These values are the guiding principles that dictate professional behaviour and action. Many organisations require members to agree to a Code of Conduct and these beliefs are likely to be outlined in such documents.

Corporate accreditation – see also Academic accreditation

    Accreditation of a corporate entity(ies) or organisation

Corporate culture

    The set of important assumptions that members of the organisation share. It is a system of shared values about what is important and beliefs about how the organisation works. These common assumptions influence the way the organisation operates.

Corporate membership model – see also Group membership

    Membership is held by an organisation or employer and is paid for by the organisation rather than by an individual while certain benefits and services are conferred on a number of the organisation's staff. This type of scheme can and regularly does complement membership schemes for individuals.

Corporate social responsibility (CSR)

    An organisation's sense of responsibility towards the community and environment (both ecological and social) in which it operates. Organisations express this involvement through their waste and pollution reduction processes; by contributing educational and social programmes and by earning adequate returns on the employed resources. These activities have recently been shown to enhance employee work satisfaction and engagement.

Corrective action

    The implementation of solutions resulting in the reduction or elimination of an identified problem.

COTS systems (Commercial-Off-the-Shelf)

    Commercial-off-the-shelf (COTS) software and services are usually built and delivered from a third party vendor. COTS systems can be purchased, leased or even licensed to organisations or the general public and typically require configuration that is tailored for specific uses.

Council
>Traditionally membership organisations and professional associations have been governed by their councils (previously the most senior formally constituted body within organisations). More recently there has been a trend to move strategic decision making responsibility to newly formed (and streamlined) Trustee Boards and leave councils to debate on organisational stance, overall direction and/or subject specific intent.

CPD – see Continuing professional development
>Continuing professional development (CPD) is the means by which individuals maintain their knowledge and skills, related to their professional lives, through professional learning and development over the full length of their career.

CPD requirement – see also Revalidation
>Many professional associations and membership organisations require members to conduct continuing professional development and may set a specific requirement. Measurement tools may include a set number of points or hours per year (Inputs), completion of a Portfolio or peer to peer dialogue (Outputs/Outcomes).

CPD Schemes
>CPD Schemes enable associations and membership organisations to measure or monitor members' continuing professional development (CPD) activity, often via annual declarations from members. Scheme types vary from input-based schemes (hours/points), output-based schemes (goal focused) or outcome-based schemes (competency focused). The schemes also vary between industries, sectors and professions as to whether this activity is voluntary or obligatory/ mandatory.

CPE – see Constant professional engagement

Cradle-to-grave – see also Young members and Retired members
>A term which refers to the end to end member journey and the

individual's long term relationship with the organisation. It will normally be linked to career and/or life stages for individual members, e.g. student, associate, member, fellow.

Creative intelligence

A vital dimension of the human capacity for knowing and learning, fostered through understanding of how the creative process works and how to apply it.

Crisis management

The process by which an association or membership organisation deals with a major event that threatens to harm the organisation, its members, stakeholders, and/or the general public. Activities and discussions will usually happen on a daily or weekly basis but may be much longer term.

Criteria

A means or standard of assessing suitability.

Critical friend

A trusted person who asks provocative questions, provides data to be examined through another lens, and offers critiques of a person's work as a friend. A critical friend takes the time to fully understand the context of the work presented and the outcomes that the person or group is working toward. The friend is an advocate for the success of that work.

Critical or key variables

A variable in common between two datasets, which may therefore be used for linking records between them.

CRM system – see also Membership database

The software system used to manage effective relationships, interactions, knowledge, financial transactions, data and information of non-members, members organisations and key stakeholders.

CRM Provider
Usually commercial providers of a CRM software solution.

Crowdfunding
The practice of funding a project or venture by raising many small amounts of money from a large number of people, typically via the Internet.

Crowdlending
A way in which people, organisations, and businesses (including start-ups) can raise money through online portals (crowdlending platforms) to finance or refinance their activities. It provides a platform for individuals who are looking for a return on their investment with businesses that need finance at a sensible price, cutting out the banking middle-men in the process.

CSR – see Corporate Social Responsibility

Culture – see also Organisational culture
Culture represents the shared expectations and self-image of the organisation. The mature values that create 'tradition', the 'feel' of the organisation over time and the deep, unwritten code that frames 'how we do things around here' all contribute to the culture. Organisational culture is a system of shared values, assumptions, beliefs and norms that unite the members of the organisation or contribute to its problems. Changing or creating cultures can be incredibly difficult and time consuming.

Customer relationship
The relationship that the professional association or membership organisation has with its members, non-members and stakeholders while providing services.

Customer relationship management (CRM)
CRM is a term often used to describe the relationship between the organisation and its member(s). It also used as a shorthand name for a membership database. More advanced approaches to CRM incorporate the effective management of relationships,

interactions, knowledge, financial transactions, and other historical data. Typically organisations hold information on non-members, members, organisations and key stakeholders. CRM is undoubtedly a structured approach to membership management; however deeper approaches that incorporate engagement, behavioural and social analysis are now coming to the fore.

Customer service

The provision of service to customers before, during and after a purchase. A series of activities designed to enhance the level of customer satisfaction – that is, the feeling that a product or service has met or exceeded the customer expectation.

D

Dashboards – see also Balanced scorecards

Real-time data intelligence used to inform decision making and to shape strategy. Often utilising RAG reports (see entry) and provided in a graphic format for ease of use.

Data Protection Act – see also ICO (Information Commissioner's Office)

The Data Protection Act 1998 (DPA) defines UK law on the processing of data on identifiable living people. It controls how personal information is used by organisations, businesses or the government and stipulates that everyone using data has the responsibility to follow strict rules known as 'data protection principles'.

Data protection officer / Data protection compliance officer

An individual who is appointed to advise on the implications of data protection law and develop the membership organisation or association's privacy and data protection policies.

DDA (Disability Discrimination Act)

The Disability Discrimination Act (DDA) 1995 was introduced to end the discrimination faced by many people with physical or mental disabilities. The Act has been significantly extended, including the Disability Discrimination (NI) Order 2006 (DDO). The legislation requires all organisations to promote equality of opportunity for people with disabilities.

Death by Powerpoint

A business colloquialism describing a phenomenon caused by the poor use of presentation software. Normally caused by overlong, wordy and boring presentations in Powerpoint or other software, used by presenters with little or no competence in relation to delivering presentations resulting in extreme boredom or inattention by the audience.

Decision matrix

A matrix used by teams to evaluate possible solutions to problems. Each solution is listed. Criteria are then selected and listed across the top row to rate the possible solutions. Each possible solution is rated on a scale from 1 to 5 for each criterion and the rating recorded in the corresponding grid. The ratings of all the criteria for each possible solution are added to determine each solution's score. The scores are then used to help decide which solution deserves the most attention.

De-dupe

To remove duplicate entries from a list, spreadsheet or database.

Defaulter

One who fails to renew their annual membership subscription.

Deficiency

Failure to meet a set performance standard.

Delegate

- A name given to an individual who chooses to attend a membership organisation event or conference.
- This term can also refer to a person chosen or elected by a group to attend, speak or vote at a meeting, event or conference. A group of delegates in this instance is recognised as a delegation.

Delegated Authority - see also Empowerment

An individual, usually a manager, may not be able to perform all the tasks assigned to them. In order to complete the work on time, the manager may be able to delegate authority, usually to a subordinate, and entrust them to complete the specified tasks. The manager is still responsible for the delegated tasks and must ensure that they are achieved effectively and deliver the results expected.

Delegation

- The assignment of responsibility or authority to another person (normally from a manager to a subordinate) to carry out specific activities. The person who delegates the work remains accountable for the outcome of the delegated work.
- A group of delegates to an event or conference attending on behalf of others.

Deliverables

A tangible or intangible object produced as a result of a project or programme that is intended to be delivered to the customer or member.

Demographic – see also Membership demographic

A single statistic or set of statistical information ordinarily relating to either a population, a trade or industry, membership of a particular sector or a profession.

Dependency / Dependencies

The relationship between conditions, events or tasks such that one cannot begin or be completed until one or more other conditions, events or tasks have occurred, begun or been completed. Of particular importance in the planning and delivery of projects and programmes.

Depreciation

In accountancy, depreciation refers to the decrease in value of tangible assets and the allocation of the cost of assets to periods in which the assets are used.

Designated fund – see also Restricted fund

Designated funds are charitable contribution with the stipulation that they must be used for a specified purpose, e.g. a particular project or initiative.

Designatory letters– see also Post-nominal letters

These are letters placed after the name of a person to indicate that the individual holds a position, educational degree, accreditation, office or honour. An individual may use several different sets of post-nominal letters. The order in which these are listed after a name is based on the order of precedence and category of the order.

Desk research – see also Field research

Sometimes referred to as secondary research, this process involves accessing sources of information (usually text-based) such as reports, journals, etc, to summarise, collate and synthesise existing research rather than conducting Primary research. This may serve as the starting point to conduct further field research or to decide if further research is required.

Digital-only membership model –see also Virtual member

A membership proposition providing members with a digital-only membership and/or online member benefits. An example might be free student membership in which benefits are only delivered and received online.

Direct costs

Costs that are directly attributable to an activity; the effort, material or equipment costs, as opposed to the Indirect costs (see entry).

Direct Debit mandate (DDM)

Direct Debit mandates provide membership organisations and professional associations in the UK permission to take payments from the accounts of individuals or organisations (members/ non-members) at agreed intervals (usually monthly, quarterly or annually). Ordinarily a mandate will be used to pay for membership subscription fees.

Direct Debit payments

Payments made via the Direct Debit scheme in the UK by individuals or organisations at agreed intervals (usually monthly, quarterly or annually).

Director
>An individual who is a member of the governing group of a company or institution who may or may not have an executive function but who will direct the affairs of the organisation.

Director General – see Chief Executive Officer
>A title given to the highest executive officer within an organisation. See also Chief Executive Officer and Secretary General.

Disability – see DDA

Disciplinary committee
>An independent committee, sometimes derived as a subset of a larger advisory or standing committee, which conducts disciplinary proceedings arising from complaints about members relating to serious breaches in professionalism or legal requirements. If a professional Code of conduct (see entry) is in place then this committee will ordinarily establish if a breach has occurred and then decide on the consequences of that breach. Most disciplinary committees have the authority to recommend a range of sanctions including suspension or disqualification of members.

Disciplinary procedure
>A set of clearly defined processes and procedures by which the organisation deals administratively with disciplinary hearings, usually by arranging a meeting of the Disciplinary committee.

Discounting membership fees
>Discounted membership fees can be applied in various circumstances and can be applied formally (e.g. student membership) or informally depending on circumstance.

Discretionary
>Available at the discretion of the membership organisation or professional association.

Dissolution
>The process for formally ending or winding down a legal entity, e.g. dissolve a professional association or membership organisation.

Diversity
>Committing to establish an environment where the full potential of all employees and/or members can be assisted by paying attention to, and taking into account, their differences in work background, experience, age, gender, race, ethnic origin, physical abilities, religious belief, sexual orientation, and other differences.

Due diligence
>A term which can be defined in two ways:
>- The care that a reasonable person exercises to avoid harm to other persons or their property.
>- Research and analysis of a company or organisation done in preparation for a business transaction (perhaps a corporate merger or purchase of securities).

Dues – see also Subscription fees
>An alternative description for annual subscription fee (used in the US and Canada).

E

e-books

An electronic version of a printed book that can be read on a computer or handheld electronic device (tablet) designed specifically for this purpose. Books are increasingly being produced in this form only without the corresponding production of a hard copy version.

Effectiveness

The degree to which something or someone (e.g. a member) is successful in producing a desired result. In most cases the professional association or membership organisation should have a positive impact on an individual or organisational members' effectiveness and competence.

Efficiency

A measure (usually as a percentage) of the actual output compared to the standard output expected. Efficiency measures how well an individual or an organisation is performing relative to expectations.

EGM – see Extraordinary general meeting

eLearning – see also Blended learning and Online learning

Refers to the use of electronic media and information and communication technologies (ICT) in education. It includes delivery via numerous types of media and processes that deliver text, audio, images, animation, and streaming video. It can occur in or out of the classroom, can be self-paced, asynchronous learning or may be instructor-led, synchronous learning. e-Learning is suited to distance and flexible learning but it can also be used in conjunction with face-to-face teaching, in which case the term blended learning is commonly used.

Elections – see also Voting

Membership organisation or professional association elections provide members with the opportunity to vote for a person to hold an official role or position, e.g. Chair, President, Treasurer, Council member.

Email marketing / Email management
Use of a professional email marketing tool to send out one-off member communications and regular member eUpdates. These tools provide professional self-service functionality and useful analytics to monitor or audit readership and interest.

Emerging membership models
Membership models are constantly evolving and changing. This term refers to this phenomenon in creating new types of membership.

Empathy
The capacity to recognise emotions that are being experienced by another person. An extremely useful competence for all staff to develop so that they are able to understand both each other and how members might feel when using the organisation's services or experiencing a particular interaction with members of staff.

Employee engagement - see also Staff engagement and Corporate social responsibility
A workplace approach designed to ensure that employees are committed to their organisation's goals and values, motivated to contribute to organisational success, and are able at the same time to enhance their own sense of well-being.

Employee protection – see Whistleblower policy
Protection of the rights of workers in a company or organisation, for example the right for women to go on maternity leave or the right to be given a reasonable redundancy payment. Employment protection also refers to the system of laws, agreements, and processes that make this possible.

Employment law
The area of law that covers all aspects of the legal rights and duties of employers and employees and their relationships. Most employment laws have been established to protect the rights of employees.

Empowerment – see also Delegated authority
A condition whereby employees have the authority to make decisions and take action in their work areas, jobs or tasks without prior approval. It allows the employees to exercise some responsibility within their role.

EMS (Engagement management system)
Software which manages all member data and relevant web content in one system, providing personalised web experience and enhanced connection for members. Used to enable (via personalisation) and measure (via analytics) the levels of engagement between a membership organisation or association and its members.

e-newsletters – see also Click through rate, Open rate and Mailing house and Email marketing
e-newsletters are sent by membership organisations and associations to various audiences (e.g. members, non-members) and can be sent for various purposes, e.g. monthly updates, regional updates, membership segment-specific purposes and special interests.

Enforcement / Enforcement bodies – see also Regulatory body
A regulatory body (or regulatory authority, regulatory agency or regulator) is a body formed or mandated under the terms of a legislative act or statute to ensure compliance with the provisions of the act, and in carrying out its purpose. An independent regulatory agency is independent from other branches or arms of government. Some independent regulatory agencies perform investigations or audits and some are authorised to fine the relevant parties and order certain measures when shortcomings are established beyond question.

Engagement

> Creating an emotional connection between either an employee and their employer or between an organisation, its members, stakeholders and potential members. The engagement tends to influence behaviours and levels of effort in work or brand related behaviours such as advocacy and participation in activities.

Engagement management – see also Member engagement management (MEM)

> The management of member engagement in a planned and structured manner, e.g.
> via the use of an Engagement management system (EMS).

Engagement management system – see EMS

Environmental scan – see also PEST or PESTLE analysis

> Examination of the political, strategic, operational or sectoral context within which the organisation operates.

ePortfolio - see also Revalidation

> Many membership organisations and associations (particularly professional bodies) provide members with the opportunity to collect electronic evidence of CPD, assembled and managed by a user, usually on the Web. Such electronic evidence may include inputted text, electronic files, images, multimedia, blog entries and hyperlinks. ePortfolios are both demonstrations of the user's competence and platforms for self-expression, and, if they are online, may be maintained dynamically over time. Many are assessed or moderated either formally or informally and within a growing number of professions and trades are completed in order to practice.

Escalation

> An increase in the intensity or seriousness of something; an intensification. A method for passing decisions upwards through the internal decision-making hierarchy.

ESOL (English for speakers of other languages or English as a second or other language)

> English language courses or learning programmes produced specifically for native speakers of other languages.

Estimating

> The process of combining the results of experience, metrics and measurements to arrive at an approximate judgement of time, cost and resource requirements of an activity or project.

Evaluation

> Judging the worth, quality or significance of people, ideas or things.

Event oriented membership model

> In this model membership may form a secondary value-added and inclusive benefit of attending a particular paid-for conference or event.

eWallet integration

> A number of membership organisations and professional associations are providing eWallet functionality for members. This enables members to store 'virtual money' and use it to spend on products and services.

Exclusivity

> A number of membership organisations and professional associations promote products and service as exclusively available to members. This should form part of the organisation's Member value proposition (MVP) (see entry) and contributes directly towards member engagement, member recruitment and retention.

Executive committee – see also Board of directors

> Group of directors appointed to act on behalf of, and within the powers granted to them by, the Board of directors. Typically it consists of a chairperson, vice-chairperson, secretary and treasurer.

Executive summary

An executive summary is a short document or section of a document or committee paper that summarises the full report, proposal, paper or a group of related reports in such a way that the reader can quickly become acquainted with a large body of material without having to read it all.

Exhibition / Trade exhibition

Many associations and membership organisations that hold a national conference may also hold an exhibition (or trade exhibition) alongside. Stand space is sold to exhibitors as an additional source of income. Exhibitors may include suppliers relevant to members' needs and requirements, organisations that wish to lobby to delegates, related charities and/or information poster or competition sections.

Exit interview / Exit survey – see also Leavers' survey

A survey conducted with an individual who is leaving an organisation. Most commonly, this occurs between an employee and an organisation or a member and an association. The organisation can then use the information gained from exit interviews to assess what should be improved, changed, or remain intact.

Ex-officio

A member of a body (a Board, Committee, Council, etc) who is part of it by virtue of their skills external to the organisation or holding other office. Their rights are usually limited by the By-laws of a particular body. Frequently, ex officio members will abstain from voting, but unless by-laws constrain their rights, they are afforded the same rights as other members, including debate or making formal motions. By-laws quite often provide that the organisation's President will be an ex officio member of all committees, except the Nominations committee.

Expert witness

A person whose level of specialised knowledge or skill in a particular field qualifies them to present their opinion about the facts of a case during legal proceedings.

Expression of interest (EOI)
> This common commissioning term defines a process in the commissioning cycle in which an organisation formally expresses an interest in bidding for a contract, usually by way of a short application form.

Extraordinary general meeting (EGM) - see also Annual general meeting (AGM)
> An extraordinary general meeting of at least a Quorum (see entry) of the members of an organisation under company law to deal with important subjects which cannot wait until the next Annual general meeting.

Extrinsic
> Not contained within or belonging to a particular body or organisation, as opposed to Intrinsic (see entry).

F

Facilitator
>An individual, probably external to the organisation, who helps a group of people understand their common objectives and assists them to plan to achieve them without taking a particular position in the discussion. Some facilitator tools will try to assist the group in achieving a consensus on any disagreements that may pre-exist or emerge in the meeting so that it has a strong basis for future action. May also be utilised for Brainstorming or envisioning activities. Sometimes referred to as facilitation workshops.

Facilities management - see also Health and safety policy and Property asset management
>The management of facilities ordinarily based within the organisation HQ and/or regional office infrastructure. Examples may include physical health and safety requirements, room booking, telephone lines and postage. This management requirement is sometimes outsourced.

Faculties – see also Sections
>This term is used by a number of membership organisations and professional associations to identify a local branch or section of the organisation probably with specific interests. This function is critical to optimising local member value and engagement and is likely to provide a range of services, e.g. local newsletter, events and networking opportunities.

FAQs – see Frequently asked questions

Federation
>A group of membership organisations or professional associations that have joined together to form a larger, usually representative, organisation or governing body.

Fee remission
> The process by which an individual member is allowed to not pay monies they they would normally owe, e.g. their membership fee, usually because of unusual or extenuating circumstances.

Feedback – see also Member feedback
> The flow of information back to the individual or organisation so that actual performance can be compared with planned performance.

Fellows
> Fellows are usually the highest grade of membership of most professional or learned societies. Lower grades include, among others, Members (who typically share voting rights with the fellows), or Associates (who may or may not, depending on whether associate status is a form of full membership), Licentiates.

Fellowship committee
> A committee with the responsibility for criteria and development of this grade of membership and may also be responsible for assessment in some organisations.

Field research – see also Desk research
> The collection of information outside of a laboratory or workplace setting. Field research involves a range of well-defined, although variable, methods: informal interviews, direct observation, participation in the life of the group, collective discussions, analyses of personal documents produced within the group, self-analysis, results from activities undertaken off- or on-line, and life-histories. Although the method generally is characterised as qualitative research, it may (and often does) include quantitative dimensions.

File transfer and FTP
> File transfer is the movement of one or more files from one location to another. The File Transfer Protocol (FTP) is a common

way to transfer a single file or a relatively small number of files from one computer to another. For larger file transfers (a single large file or a large collection of files), file compression and aggregation into a single archive is commonly used. A zip file is a popular implementation.

Finance committee

A committee responsible for the association or membership organisation's finances and financial regulation. Most committees are chaired by the organisation's Treasurer and/or Finance Director.

Financial forecast

A forecast of the expected financial position and the results of operations and cash flows based on expected conditions.

Financial strategy – see also Budgeting

A financial strategy is adopted by an organisation to pursue its economic objectives. In this context, formulating a financial strategy is the responsibility of top leadership, although department heads and finance departments will also contribute. Adequate financial planning enables an organisation to set the short-term operating framework necessary to achieve long-term results.

Finding of no significant impact (FONSI)

A finding of no significant impact (FONSI) identifies the reasons why an action will not have a significant effect on the organisation's environment or operations.

Fit-for-purpose

Something that is appropriate and of a necessary standard for its intended use, i.e. is good enough to do the job it was designed to do.

Fixed assets

These are long-term, tangible assets held for business use and not expected to be converted to cash in the current or upcoming financial year. Buildings, real estate, equipment and furniture are good examples of fixed assets. Generally, intangible long-term assets such as trademarks and patents are not categorised as fixed assets but are more specifically referred to as fixed intangible assets.

Fixed renewals – see also Annual renewals

This membership scheme model requires all members to renew on a set date or within a specific time period, usually on an annual basis. This is probably one of the oldest paid-for membership scheme models in existence and can be referred to as annual renewal.

Flexibility

The ability of a system or an individual to respond quickly, in terms of range and time, to external or internal changes or pressures.

Flexible working - see also Flexitime and TOIL (Time off in lieu)

Flexitime - see also Home working

An arrangement in which employees are allowed to choose work hours to suit their personal circumstances as long as the standard or contracted number of work hours are met. Some flexitime systems require that the hours fall within a certain range of hours and some treat the arrangement as outsourcing.

Focus group

A form of qualitative research in which a group of people are asked about their perceptions, opinions, beliefs, and attitudes towards a product, service, concept, advertisement, idea, or packaging. Questions are asked in an interactive, structured and moderated group setting where participants are free to talk with other group members.

FONSI - see Finding of no significant impact

Force majeure

A common clause in contracts that frees both parties from liability or obligation when an extraordinary event or circumstance beyond the control of the parties occurs. Examples include war, riot, strikes, crime or an environment event outside their control which prevents one or both parties from fulfilling their obligations under the contract. In practice, most force majeure clauses do not excuse a party's non-performance entirely but only suspends it for the duration of the force majeure.

Forecasting

The use of historic data to determine the direction of future trends. Forecasting is used by companies to determine how to allocate their budgets for an upcoming period of time. This is typically based on demand for the goods and services it offers, compared to the cost of producing them.

Founder member

An individual who has helped to establish a new organisation, club etc and is one of its first members. They often remain involved in a volunteer capacity for a very long time.

Free market

A market economy based on supply and demand with little or no government control. A completely free market is an idealised form of market economy where buyers and sellers are allowed to transact freely (i.e. buy/sell/trade) based on a mutual agreement on price without state intervention in the form of taxes, subsidies or regulation. In financial markets, free market stocks are securities that are widely traded and whose prices are not affected by availability. In foreign-exchange markets, it is a market where exchange rates are not pegged (by government) and thus rise and fall freely though supply and demand for currency.

Freemium model of membership

This type of membership model enables free membership

but money is charged for further products, services, tools and resources, e.g. conference attendance and eLearning opportunities.

Frequently asked questions (FAQs)

A document or web page, in question and answer format, that introduces newcomers to a particular topic. A list that provides answers to questions commonly asked by visitors new to a service or website.

Friends membership scheme

This type of membership is used by organisations wishing to provide an offering for individuals or organisations that may not fit core membership criteria or grades. In return for an annual fee or donation individuals are typically invited to attend lectures, visits, dinners and/or have access to discounted services.

FTP – see File transfer protocol

Full member

Full members ordinarily meet all the criteria of membership. Some organisations may provide the opportunity to upgrade to Fellow/Fellowship.

Full time equivalent (FTE)

A measure showing how many employees an organisation has or a project requires assuming all employees work a full-time schedule. FTE is a helpful measurement because it helps budget analysts and project managers estimate labour cost. By knowing how many people are needed to accomplish certain tasks and at the approximate salary, budgets can be set to complete the work. While it often does, one FTE does not necessarily equal one job vacancy. Part-time employees sharing a job can equal one FTE, and some jobs do not require a full FTE.

Fundraising membership scheme

This type of membership is driven by the desire to 'donate' and is usually found in charitable donation-based organisations or charities. Donation payments are often made in instalments and, in return, members are likely to receive a welcome pack explaining what their donations will achieve and regular updates or publications throughout the year to maintain engagement.

Fundraising committee

Committee responsible for the fundraising activities of an organisation. Typically the committee will be led by a key organisational stakeholder to ensure cross-organisation buy-in. See also Benevolent Fund.

G

Gamification

Gamification is an emerging way organisations are adopting to format online learning (eLearning) opportunities in order to engage the learner more closely. Much debate currently surrounds this area.

Gantt chart

A chart showing a list of activities, represented by bars, that are proportional in length to their duration. The bars are positioned along a horizontal time scale. Originally a project management term.

Gap analysis

This is the comparison of actual performance with potential performance. If a company or organisation does not make the best use of current resources, or foregoes investment in capital or technology, it may produce or perform below its potential.

General Manager – see also Chief Executive Officer and Secretary General

Alternative job title occasionally given to the role known as Chief Executive Officer in similar organisations. Use of this term can be misleading in terms of responsibility levels.

Generational differences – see also Silent generation, Baby boomers, Generation C, Generation X, Generation Y, Generation Z

Generation C (Gen C)

Gen C is a powerful new force in consumer culture, sometimes known as the Digital native or the You-Tube generation. A term used to describe people who care deeply about creation, curation, connection, and community. It is not strictly an age group but an attitude and mindset defined by key characteristics. Some 65% are under 35 but they span the generations, empowered by technology searching for authentic content that they consume across all platforms and all screens, whenever and wherever they want. They can be difficult to reach with traditional media but brands that take the time to understand them and properly engage with them will find a willing and influential audience.

Generation X – see also Generational differences

Generation X, commonly abbreviated to Gen X, is the generation born after the post-World War II baby boom in the West. Demographers, historians, and commentators use beginning birth dates ranging from the early 1960s to the early 1980s.

Generation Y – see also Generational differences

Millennials (also known as the Millennial Generation or Gen Y) are the demographic cohort following Generation X. There are no precise dates when the generation starts and ends but researchers and commentators use birth years ranging from the early 1980s to the early 2000s.

Generation Z – see also Generational differences

Generation Z is one name used for the cohort of people born after the Millenial Generation. There is no agreement on the exact dates of the generation with some sources starting it at the mid or late 1990s or from the mid 2000s to the present day.

Goals

The aims of the organisation, its purpose and what it wants to achieve.

Good practice – see Best practice and Industry standard

Governance

In a non-profit organisation, governance relates to consistent management, cohesive policies, guidance, processes and decision-rights for a given area of responsibility. The quality and structure of governance within the organisation is often compared with established standards of good governance to assess whether improvements are required. Governance reviews should be undertaken on a regular basis, every year for preference or once every two years if annual reviews are not feasible.

Grant giving – see also Benevolent Fund

Many associations and membership organisations provide the opportunity for members (and non-members) to apply for financial help and support. Coverage and criteria vary, however there is ordinarily a direct link back to the organisation, its charitable objects, research and/or support of those in financial need.

Green credentials

The qualities that show that individuals or organisations as a whole believe it is important to protect the natural environment.

Group membership – see also Corporate membership and Corporate accreditation

Growth

The process of improving some measure of an organisation's success. Achieved either by boosting Revenue by increasing product sales or service income, or increasing profitability by minimising costs. Enhancing reputation is a further important element of any growth plan. In the world of membership this word often refers to membership growth, however it can also refer to other areas of the organisation that are seeing increases, e.g. increases in annual conference attendee numbers.

H

Health and Safety – see also Health and safety regulations

Associations and membership organisations (like all other employers) have a duty to ensure all staff, stakeholders or the public can work or meet in a safe and healthy environment and provide products and services which meet the appropriate health and safety standards. Guidance on all aspects of Health and Safety is obtained from the Health and Safety Executive (HSE).

Health and safety policy – see also Crisis management and Facilities management

In order for associations and membership organisations to adhere to health and safety regulations, all need to have appropriate health and safety policies that are in place and actively enforced.

Health and safety regulations

The regulations linked directly to health and safety that associations and membership organisations must adhere to as employers or the providers of products and services to stakeholders and the general public.

Heuristics

Relates to a way of solving problems by finding solutions based on an individual's own experiences.

HMRC List 3

In the UK the HMRC (Her Majesty's Revenue and Customs) enables professional bodies and learned societies to register on this list and it enables members to gain tax relief on annual membership fees. This is an excellent way to provide member value by reducing the price of membership without having to provide a reduction in membership fee and therefore no effect on income levels.

Home working – see also Remote working and Flexitime

Home workers are defined by the International Labour Organisation as people working from their homes or from other premises of their choosing other than the workplace, for payment, which results in a product or service specified by the employer. Recently, the phenomenon of home working has grown with increased use of communication technology.

Honorary fellow

Appointment as an honorary fellow in a learned society or professional association can be awarded either to honour exceptional achievement and/or service within the professional domain of the awarding body or to recognise relevant contributions from someone who is professionally outside of it. Existing membership of the membership organisation or association may or may not be a requirement. Honorary members are not usually voting members and would not usually pay membership fees.

Honorary member

An honorary member is one who has been recognised as a supporter or advocate of the profession and one who has sustained a record of service. Existing membership of the membership organisation or association may or may not be a requirement. Honorary members are not usually voting members and would not usually pay membership fees.

Horizon scanning – see also Scenario development

A systematic examination of information to identify potential threats, risks, emerging issues and opportunities, allowing for better preparedness and the incorporation of mitigation and exploitation into the decision making process.

Hump – see also Annual hump

Sometimes known as the membership peak.

I

I and E – see also Income and expenditure accounting
>The equivalent in an accounting entity that is not a business
enterprise of a profit and loss account. An income and
expenditure account shows how the excess of expenditure over
income or surplus of income over expenditure is computed
starting with income. In the Companies Act, any reference to a
profit and loss account is taken, in the case of a company not
trading for profit, as referring to its income and expenditure
account.

ICO (Information Commissioner's Office) - see also Data Protection
>The ICO is an independent Regulatory body (see entry)
providing advice and guidance about data protection and
freedom of information. The Data Protection Act 1998 requires
every organisation that processes personal information to
register with the Information Commissioner's Office (ICO),
unless they are exempt. Failure to do so is a criminal offence.

IiP – see also Investors in People and Accreditation
>Investors in People (IiP) is a nationally recognised framework
that helps organisations to improve their performance and
realise their objectives through the effective management and
development of their people. The standard is based on three
key principles:
>- Plan – Developing strategies to improve the performance of
the organisation
>- Do – Taking action to improve the performance of the
organisation
>- Review – Evaluating the impact on the performance of the
organisation.

Impact report
>A growing number of membership organisations and
professional associations are publishing this type of report
to demonstrate that the organisation (and its membership)

are actioning real change or development and providing members and stakeholders with value. Typically this document is either stand-alone or is published with (or as part of) the organisation's annual report and can contribute directly towards improved member and stakeholder engagement.

Inactive member – see also Lapsed member

A member who chooses not to participate or is not able to maintain current membership because of unemployment, illness or other circumstances but remains within the membership listings of the organisation.

Incentivising

In the membership world incentivising is ordinarily linked to membership recruitment and retention (communicating the value of membership) or incentivising the purchase of related products and services, e.g. a discounted conference early-bird ticket.

Inclusivity

Most associations and membership organisations now take a more inclusive approach, e.g. ensuring board membership is diverse, making products and services fully accessible to differently abled individuals and broadening fellowship criteria.

Income and expenditure accounting - see also I and E

Income – see also Turnover

Money that an individual or organisation receives in exchange for providing products or services or through investing capital. Income is usually consumed to deal with day-to-day expenditure.

Independent adjudicator (IA)

During arbitration processes or commercial disputes, an independent adjudicator brings disputing parties together to resolve their difference of opinion.

Independent assessor

> An independent assessor is appointed, usually by a qualifications, certification or accreditation board, to take an independent view on whether an individual or organisation has met pre-determined and published criteria or standards.

Independent verifier (IV)

> An individual who is appointed to ensure that an accredited individual or organisation continues to maintain awarded criteria or standards.

Indirect costs

> Overhead costs associated with an activity or project which cannot be directly attributed to any activity or discrete group of activities, e.g. the cost of administration.

Individual member

> The phrase used to identify members as individuals as opposed to other types of members, e.g. corporate members.

Induction – see also Orientation

> All staff and volunteers, including board members, should undergo a comprehensive induction process when joining the organisation to introduce them to the requirements of their own roles, as well as the organisation and its various requirements and ways of working. An especially important process if an individual has no prior experience of the membership sector as working practices are unique compared with other sectors.

Industrial and provident society (IPS)

> A legal form of governance structure for a trading business or voluntary organisation in the United Kingdom, Republic of Ireland and New Zealand. UK legal developments include the Co-operatives and Community Benefit Societies Act 2003, which has introduced the concept of an asset lock, which a society registered as a community benefit society (but not one registered as a co-operative) can introduce to prevent specified

assets being used for unintended purposes. An IPS may in general conduct any legal business except that of investment for profit.

Industry standard – see also Best practice and Good practice
Recognised and/or determined practices and processes that are known to deliver positive or optimal results. A method or technique that has consistently shown results superior to those achieved with other means, and that is used as a benchmark. Best practice can evolve to become better as improvements are discovered. Used to describe the process of developing and following a standard way of doing things that multiple organisations can use. Best practices are used to maintain quality as an alternative to mandatory legislated standards and can be based on self-assessment or benchmarking. A feature of accredited management standards such as ISO 9000 (Quality management) and ISO 14001 (Environmental management).

Influence and negotiation

Ways in which to get other people to see things slightly differently or to get them to do something you need them to by utilising interpersonal and communication skills in order to get other people to want to give you their support. Negotiation is a tool that assists parties to obtain an agreement based on their interests, but ultimately, what we do when we negotiate is to attempt to influence others to accept our way. Negotiation is measured by two criteria: Results and effects on relationships. A successful negotiation happens when we achieve our objectives in terms of results and keep the relationship, at least, within cooperative limits.

Information commissioner - see ICO

Information management

The collection and management of information from one or more sources and the distribution of that information to one or more audiences. This sometimes involves those who have a stake in, or a right to, that information.

Information service

Simply described as a service which provides data, knowledge and information. Also any combination of information technology and people's activities using that technology to support operations, management, and decision-making. Frequently used to refer to the interaction between people, algorithmic processes, data and technology.

Inputs – see also Outcomes and Outputs

Something put into a system or expended in its operation to achieve output or a result.

Instalment payments

Subscription payment options enable associations and membership organisations to charge members via instalments. Typically these are monthly or quarterly, e.g. Direct Debit, PayPal or recurring credit card payments.

Institute

The term "institute" is a protected word and appears on the 'Sensitive words' list from Companies House. Companies or other organisations may only use the word if they are "organisations which are carrying out research at the highest level or professional bodies of the highest standing".

Insurance

Many organisations provide insurance products to their members and in some cases this can provide a great Unique selling point (USP) from a recruitment and retention perspective. Examples include professional indemnity insurance (PII), business insurance, event insurance and home or travel insurance. See also Affinity membership scheme.

Insurance membership model

A membership model where provision of professional insurance or indemnity leads the membership proposition. Supplementary member benefits may enhance this offering, e.g. free access to tools and resources.

Integrated reporting

A concise communication about how an organisation's strategy, governance, performance and prospects, in the context of its external environment, lead to the creation of value in the short, medium and long term. The integrated representation of a company's performance in terms of both financial and other value relevant information provides greater context for the data, clarifies how value relevant information fits into operations or the business plan, and may help embed long-term thinking into an organisation's decision making.

Integrity

A moral virtue that encompasses the sum total of a person's set of values and moral code. A breach of any of these values will damage the integrity of the individual. Integrity also entails the consistent adherence of action to one's personal moral beliefs. Can also be said to apply to the organisation as a whole.

Intellectual Property Rights (IPR) – see also Copyright and Performing Rights

The legal rights a person or company has to the ownership of their ideas, designs, and inventions, including copyrights, patents and trademarks.

Interdependencies

In the membership world a number of activities carry interdependencies when departments must rely on one another to share information, financial resources, etc, making interpersonal communication highly valuable and necessary for a successful outcome. Interdependencies exist when the actions of one department affect important outcomes in another area. Some will be simple and straight-forward (e.g. estimating the total number of members who will upgrade to fellowship in any year and estimating both the effort required and the potential increase in subscriptions) and others may be more complex (e.g. calculating the following year's membership subscription income following a decision to increase the membership fee).

Internal verifier
> The primary role of an internal verifier is to monitor the work of all assessors involved with a qualification, to ensure that they are applying the assessment criteria consistently throughout all assessment activities.

International membership / Global membership / Overseas membership
> Within this membership grade, members typically reside outside the country where the organisation is located. Fees for these members generally depend on the level of benefits and services the organisation is able to offer remotely. Some organisations maintain overseas offices if warranted.

Interpersonal skills - see also Soft Skills
> The set of abilities enabling an individual to interact positively and work effectively with others including colleagues, members, committee members and other volunteers, stakeholders and the general public. Development of the interpersonal skills of employees is a key goal of training and development initiatives for many organisations. These skills include the areas of communication, listening, delegation of tasks and leadership.

Intranet
> A private network that is contained within an organisation, often being the default opening screen on all employee's computers. The main purpose of an intranet is to share company information and access to information among employees. Sometimes, the term refers only to the organisation's internal website, but may be a more extensive part of the organisation's information technology infrastructure. The objective is to organise each individual's desktop with minimal cost, time and effort to be more productive and efficient.

Intrinsic
> Entirely contained within or belonging to a particular body or organisation, as opposed to Extrinsic (see entry).

Investment appraisal – see Capital budgeting

Investors in People – see IiP

Invitation to tender (ITT) – see also Tendering process
>Organisations are invited to submit a formal, detailed application in an attempt to win a contract. All bids received are examined against a pre-agreed set of criteria to decide which company will win the tender and carry out the work.

IPR – see Intellectual Property Rights, Copyright and Performing Rights

ITT - see Invitation to tender

J

Jobs board

A jobs board is a physical or virtual area that lists available jobs. The rise in popularity of web based boards has led to a reduction in popularity of classified ads in newspapers. In most major fields, there are websites devoted specifically to searches within that profession. From a candidate's perspective, a job board is a place to look for a job. From an employer's perspective, it's an advertising and publicity vehicle. For membership organisations and professional associations see www.membershipjobs.com.

Join

To enter into or register for membership and changing status from a non-member or nob-subscriber to a member or subscriber.

Joint venture (JV)

Associations or membership organisations may partner with other organisations and/or third party companies in order to deliver new or improved products and services. Joint ventures are one of a range of options, others being profit-share, licensing, and franchising.

Journal

Journals are published by professional associations and membership organisations on a regular basis (e.g. monthly/ quarterly) and sent to members, usually as an inclusive benefit of membership. They may also be called trade magazines, depending on content type.

Journal/magazine subscription membership model

Some organisations place emphasis on the print or digital journal/magazine. Primary research indicates the prevailing use of the word 'subscriber' in this model rather than member and unsurprisingly this model is used by a number of leading publishers. Supplementary online benefits may include member-area access for digital downloads and exclusive offers or discounts.

K

Key data

Associations and membership organisations collect data from members for a wide range of reasons although some types of data are deemed to be more important than others. Important data is known as key data, e.g. first name, last name and email address.

Key performance indicator (KPI); Key performance target (KPT) – see also Targets

Key performance indicators are quantifiable measurements that are critical to the success of a company. These indicators vary between organisations and sectors but should always, if implemented and monitored correctly, help a business define and measure progress toward both short-term and long-term organisational goals.

Key variables

An input factor in a process that has been determined to be a source of variability in the output of the process. Once the key variables are determined, statistical experiments can be designed that can reveal optimal values for each factor to achieve desired output quality.

KISS principle – keep it simple, stupid!

An acronym for "Keep it simple, stupid" as a design principle noted by the U.S. Navy in 1960. The principle states that most systems work best if they are kept simple rather than made complex; therefore simplicity should be a key goal in design and unnecessary complexity should be avoided.

Knowledge management

A range of strategies and practices used in an organisation to identify, create, represent, distribute, and enable adoption of insights and experiences which comprise knowledge, either embodied in individuals or embedded within the organisation as processes or practices.

KPI / KPT – see Key performance indicator; Key performance target – see also Targets

L

Landscape

The PEST or PESTLE (see entry) environment within which the organisation exists and within which it provides services and makes Alliances (see entry) and Partnerships (see entry).

Lapsed member - see also Inactive member

A lapsed member is usually a member who has chosen not to renew their annual membership.

Lapsed member campaign

A membership marketing campaign aimed at bringing lapsed members back into membership.

Lapsing

A member who is not proactively renewing their membership during the membership renewal period.

Lead generation

The generation of consumer interest or inquiry into products or services. Leads can be generated for purposes such as list building, e-newsletter list acquisition or for sales leads. The methods for generating leads typically fall under the umbrella of advertising, but may also include non-paid sources such as organic search engine results or referrals from existing customers. The quality of leads generated is usually determined by the propensity of the inquirer to take the next action towards a purchase.

Lead times

Lead time is the delay between the initiation and execution of a process. For example, the lead time between the planning for a new project and delivery of the expected outcomes may be anywhere from 2 months to 2 years.

Leadership

The process of influencing people while operating to meet organisational requirements and improving the organisation through change, in order to meet a common goal.

Leadership team – see also Senior management team (SMT)

A team of individuals at the highest level of the organisation who have the day-to-day responsibilities of managing the organisation.

Learned body or society

An organisation that exists to promote a particular field, discipline or profession, or a group of related disciplines or professions. Membership may be open to all, may require possession of some qualification, or may be an honour conferred by election or by invitation. Most learned societies are non-profit organisations and many act as professional bodies, regulating the activities of their members in the public interest or the collective interest of the membership.

Learning curve

A (graphical) curve reflecting the rate of improvement in performing a new task as a learner practices and uses their newly acquired skills. Often referred to during the induction and training of new members of staff or board members to bring them up to operational standard.

Learning management system (LMS)

A learning management system (LMS) is a software application for the administration, documentation, tracking, reporting and delivery of e-learning education courses or training programmes.

Learning styles

An individual's preferred or best method of gaining knowledge; their unique approach to learning based on their strengths, weaknesses and preferences.

Leavers' survey - see also Exit interview / survey

A survey carried out when members choose to leave an organisation in order to gain further understanding of their reasons for leaving. The information gleaned may eventually contribute to operational or strategic changes for the organisation.

Lessons learned – see also Post implementation review

Ordinarily the process at the end of or in relation to previous activity to examine and establish what, if any, lessons can be learned from the process and results of that activity. Reference is made to what went well, what could have worked better, what could be developed or improved if the exercise was to be repeated.

Liabilities

Debts or pecuniary obligations (as opposed to Assets – see entry).

Licentiate

The holder of a certificate of competence to practice a particular profession.

Life member – see also Retired member

A number of membership organisations and professional associations reward long standing members with the opportunity to gain life member status. Although schemes vary, most provide this in return for a one-off fee that provides inclusive membership for the lifetime of the member. This usually follows a period of maintained membership over a certain number of years.

Life fellow or Life fellowship - see also Life member

A life member is a full, voting member of an organisation who is exempt from further membership fees, usually having paid a single, lifetime payment. Life fellowship may also be conferred by the organisation as reward for many years of service.

Limited company

A type of company that offers limited liability or legal protection for its shareholders but that places certain restrictions on its ownership. These restrictions are defined in the company's bylaws or regulation.

Limited liability partnership

A legal form of governance structure in which limited partners enjoy limited personal liability while general partners (who may be individuals or organisations) have unlimited personal liability.

LinkedIn

A social networking website for people in professional occupations. Founded in December 2002 and launched in May 2003, it is mainly used for professional networking. Membership bodies use LinkedIn as part of their Social media strategy (see entry), either as a way of creating networks for their members or promoting their organisations to attract new members, e.g. by publishing research or thin pieces.

Lobbying – see also Advocacy

A form of advocacy which attempts to influence decisions made by officials in the government, most often legislators or members of regulatory agencies. Lobbying is carried out by many different types of people and organised groups, including individuals in the private sector, corporations, fellow legislators or government officials, or advocacy groups (interest groups).

Local member networks – see also Branch network, Branch structure and Chapters

A term used for particular and often structured regional groups/branches. These are often governed by local committees comprising a Chair (often elected to a national board or Council), Secretary and Treasurer. Many organisations provide limited funding (based on a per capita or member basis) and more advanced organisations require regular reporting back to HQ. Activity may include local conferences, social events and local mentoring schemes.

Logo - see also Brand

A sign, symbol or design, or a combination of them intended to identify the goods and services of one seller or group of sellers and to differentiate them from those of other sellers.

Loyalty membership scheme

This type of membership is usually focused on recurring sales of particular products or services. In return for loyalty the member receives benefits linked to the product / service, e.g. discount vouchers, free flights.

M

Macro variable – see also Horizon scanning and Scenario development
 The major external and uncontrollable factors that
 influence an organisation's decision making and affect its
 performance and strategies. These factors include economic
 factors, demographics, legal, political and social conditions;
 technological changes; and natural forces. Other specific
 examples may include competitors, changes in interest rates,
 changes in cultural tastes, disastrous weather or government
 regulations.

Magazines and journals – see also Journal, Publications and/or Trade
Journal / Magazine

Mailing house – see also e-newsletters and Mailshots
 Ordinarily an outsourced third party provider which administers
 and/or sends out hard copy publications and literature to
 members and non-members, usually via the post.

Mailshots – see also Mailing house
 A hard copy mailing, usually of a sales or marketing nature.

Management by objectives (MBO)
 A management model that aims to improve performance of an
 organisation by clearly defining objectives that are agreed to
 by both management and employees. According to the theory,
 having a say in goal setting and action plans should ensure
 better participation and commitment among employees, as well
 as alignment of objectives across the organisation. The term
 was first outlined by management guru Peter Drucker in 1954 in
 his book "The Practice of Management."

Management by walking around (MBWA)
 MBWA refers to managers spending some part of their time
 listening to problems and ideas of their staff, while wandering
 around the office or other work environment.

The term was coined by management guru Tom Peters. Apparently, from his study of successful companies and their practices, he noticed that good managers tend to communicate a lot better with their team. And they do that in informal ways, such as hanging around in the office and chatting with them, rather than having formal interaction sessions in their offices or boardrooms. Sam Walton, the founder of the largest company in the world, Walmart, was a great exponent of this practice. He believed in visiting as many of his stores as many times as possible and talking to frontline staff. The idea of this practice is to listen. Managers are then also expected to respond to ideas or problems voiced and take effective action about them. Sometimes referred to as 'back to the floor'.

Management of volunteers – see also Volunteers and Volunteer agreement
>
> The use of an agreed process by which volunteer contributions, in terms of both time and effort, are regulated by the employing organisation in order to maximise the impact the volunteer might have and to ensure that all work contributed in this way is in line with the organisation's overall strategy.

Manifesto
>
> A written statement of the beliefs, aims and policies of an organisation.

Margins
>
> The difference between the cost price and selling price of a product or service.

Market audit– see also Situational analysis
>
> A marketing audit is a comprehensive, systematic, independent, and periodic examination of a organisation's or department's marketing. It is designed to evaluate marketing assets and activities in the context of market conditions, and use the resulting analysis to aid in planning. An audit should cover both an analysis of the external situation facing the organisation and a thorough review of internal marketing goals, strategies,

capabilities, processes, and systems, and should result in
actionable recommendations.

Market intelligence
The everyday information relevant to a company or
organisation's markets, gathered and analysed specifically for
the purpose of accurate and confident decision-making in
determining market opportunity, market penetration strategy
and market development
metrics.

Market interest group – see also Special / Specific interest group
Within associations and membership organisations this term
refers to a particular subset of membership who together form
a particular market segment and might well require or welcome
specific or unique resources.

Market position(ing)
An effort to influence consumer perception of a brand or
product relative to the perception of competing brands
or products. Its objective is to occupy a clear, unique, and
advantageous position in the consumer's mind.

Market research
Any organized effort to gather information about markets or
customers and is a very important component of business
strategy. It is a key factor in maintaining competitiveness over
competitors and provides important information to identify and
analyse the market need, market size and competition.

Market saturation – see also Zero growth
A situation in which a product has become diffused (distributed)
within a market; the actual level of saturation can depend on
consumer purchasing power as well as competition, prices and
technology.

Market testing
A stage in product development where both the product and

its marketing plan are exposed to the target market in order to decide whether to reject it before its full scale launch.

Marketing plan

A marketing plan contains the activities and actions required in order to deliver a structured approach to marketing. A good marketing plan contains a clear timetable of activity and is revisited and updated periodically in line with the strategic plan.

Marketing strategy

The set of objectives which an organisation allocates to its marketing function in order to support the overall corporate strategy, together with the broad methods chosen to achieve these objectives.

Matrix working – see also Silo working

This emerging way of working has been adopted by a number of professional associations and membership organisations. This more commercially minded process enables multiple departments to work collaboratively on particular projects or programmes. Historically some organisations have operated within silo structures so this more efficient way of working helps to share the workload and skills amongst relevant individuals and departments.

Maturity (Organisational Maturity)

All organisations evolve through a series of development stages, from the point at which they are founded to the time when they have outlived their relevance or usefulness and are wound up. These stages include improving, stable, mature, stale or tired and will affect decisions about future strategy. See www.theprofessionalismgroup.co.uk

MBO – see Management by objectives

MBWA – see Management by walking around

Mediation – see also Arbitration

A settlement of a dispute or controversy by setting up an independent person between two contending parties in order to aid them in the settlement of their disagreement.

Media training

This type of training is ordinarily offered to senior stakeholders. It is particularly useful for senior officers who may not be experienced in handling the media but may be required to take part in TV or radio interviews on behalf of the organisation. It is occasionally offered to honorary officers or other senior volunteers, e.g. President, if they would be expected to offer the organisation's view on a particular issue or subject.

Meeting minutes - see also Minutes

The official written record of a meeting. Minutes may be kept by any individual in attendance at a meeting but the task is usually delegated to a specific individual. The completed document is usually distributed to all those present at the meeting and will usually also contain action points which were allocated to specific individuals.

MemArts (Memorandum and Articles of Association) - see also Constitution

In corporate governance, the articles are contained in a document which, along with the memorandum of association form the company's constitution, defines the responsibilities of the directors, the kind of business to be undertaken, and the means by which the shareholders exert control over the Board of directors.

Member

The title given (individually or collectively) to either a member or collectively to the members of a membership organisation or association.

Member benefits

In return for membership of an association or membership

organisation, a suite or collection of tangible and intangible member benefits directly related to membership are provided (inclusively or paid-for) e.g. post-nominals, discounted products and services, access to online 'Member Area'. The range of member benefits contribute directly towards the Member value propositions (MVP – see entry) for each organisation and contribute towards member engagement, member recruitment and retention activity.

Member data

The data held by the association or membership organisation relating to a member or their respective member record (contained within the organisation's Membership database/ CRM) e.g. personal details, membership subscription history, purchases or preferences.

Member discount – see also Discounting membership fees and Member rate

Membership fees can be reduced or discounted. This can be done as either a one-off promotion or applied based on specific criteria, e.g. career stage, pregnancy or financial situation.

Member engagement (ME)

The engagement of members with each other, the membership organisation or association, and the specialism, profession, or trade the organisation represents.

Member engagement management (MEM) – see also Engagement management

Member experience engineering (MEE)

This concept focuses on evaluating the membership experience and either removing negative elements of the experience or enhancing or building upon the more positive elements.

Member feedback

Feedback (quantitative and/or qualitative) which is provided by members.

Member focussed

The term used to identify activity and/or products and services aimed specifically at members.

Member personas

Detailed descriptions of so-called 'typical' members of different types. Increasing numbers of associations and membership organisations are constructing and using member personas (or predominant member groups or types) to determine future membership propositions, e.g. new member benefits, website functionality and membership marketing or communications messaging and tone.

Member rate

Ordinarily a member rate is a discounted rate (normally exclusively available to members or equivalent) for a particular product, service or initiative.

Member recruitment

The recruitment of members into the organisation, mostly new members from a population of non-members including lapsed members.

Member removal– see also Removal and Strike off

The action of removing individuals or groups of members from membership of the organisation as a result of non-payment of fees, disciplinary action or changes to the membership rules or regulations. The first instance is an administrative task but the other options require involvement of senior members of staff and/or members of the organisation's governing body, e.g. Board of trustees, Council.

Member retention

Membership organisations and associations need to effectively retain members in order to maintain member numbers. Organisations focus on improving member value and engagement to directly contribute towards improved member satisfaction and retention.

Member retention rate

Associations and membership organisations measure the rate of member retention as a percentage (e.g. 95% member retention rate) and is a key analytic which can act as a temperature-check on the health of an organisation from a membership perspective.

Member segmentation

Dividing the membership population into subsets of members who have common needs and then providing plans, strategies and related products and services that meet these needs.

Member value

The value a member gains or receives in return for membership (see Member value proposition).

Member value proposition (MVP)

A business or marketing statement that summarises why a member should buy or stay in membership. This statement should convince a potential member that an organisation's particular products or services will add more value or better solve their problems or aspirations than other potentially similar offerings. Creating a value proposition is a part of the business strategy and is based on a review and analysis of the benefits, costs and value that the organisation can deliver to its members, prospective members, and other constituent groups within and outside the organisation.

Membership card

The card issued on joining or renewing membership of a membership organisation or association. Cards can now be provided in hard copy or virtually.

Membership category

Membership categories are usually split into Voting and non-voting members. Voting members are able to vote in elections (and at general meetings if allowed to do so) whilst non-voting members are not able to vote at any time.

Membership criteria
>The entry criteria linked to gaining membership of a membership organisation or association. Many organisations have varied criteria linked to separate membership grades or categories.

Membership database – see also CRM and Engagement management system
>A tool used to collect, store and retrieve member details in a structured and secure manner. Ordinarily data is stored in two key types – individuals and/or organisations. Functionality varies and depends on a number of key factors including provider, age of software and budget.

Membership demographic – see also Demographic
>Quantifiable statistics of the population of members. These demographics can be used to place members into subsets or segments and these data subsets can be used to promote the organisation's tools and resources, market products, services and to poll opinion. Common demographics include career stage and special interest.

Membership development
>The development of membership-related strategy, planning and/or activity.

Membership/Member engagement strategy or plan
>A strategy or plan linked to improving and enhancing member engagement. Both documents should be linked to high level Membership Strategy/Planning and linked directly to elements of the organisation's strategic and operational strategies or plans to ensure a solid and robust approach.

Membership fees – see also Subscriptions and Dues
>The fee charged for membership. Ordinarily charges are made on an annual basis and are paid either by the individual, their organisation or employer.

Membership grade(s)

Associations and membership organisations may provide various grades of membership linked to, for example, fee paid or career stage. They are differentiated by specific requirements per level or grade and can provide relevant products and services (e.g. enhanced professional status and/or more comprehensive access to tools and resources). Traditional grades within a professional body may include Affiliate, Student, Associate, Member and Fellow as well as International/Overseas and Organisation.

Membership grade identity(ies) – see also Member personas

A growing number of associations and membership organisations are providing unique identities to their membership grades and the members that reside within them. This is linked to a more segmented and personalised approach that aims to improve member value and engagement. Examples of this work include the provision of icons or imagery, specific to each grade and use within grade specific events and publications.

Membership models

There are various models of membership, e.g. Freemium membership, which could be suitable for differing groups of members or different circumstances.

Membership/Member recruitment or retention strategy or plan

A strategy or plan linked to improving and enhancing member recruitment or retention. Both documents should link directly to the organisation's high level membership strategic and operational strategies and plans to ensure a solid and robust approach.

Membership report

A report setting out membership feedback and activity that can either be for internal publishing or reporting or for external use. A growing number of membership organisations and associations incorporate this in Annual reports (see entry) and

Impact reports (see entry).

Membership review

A review of membership related activity, usually with a view to making improvements. This can include membership grades, pricing, entry criteria, inclusive tools and resources, take-up and attrition.

Membership scheme

The formal schemes which professional associations and membership organisations have in place to structure and effectively manage key membership elements, including new joiner management, annual renewals administration, subscription payment administration, receipt administration, member benefit access, and the management of lapsed members.

Note: There are many types of schemes available and these are highlighted throughout this document and in the MemberWise Perfect Membership Scheme guide.

Membership strategy

Membership strategies are structured in nature but vary in format, and should almost certainly be underpinned by corporate strategy. Content will provide an overview of the current member value proposition (MVP) and how this can be developed to improve member recruitment, retention, engagement, value and growth. Typically membership strategy documents contain full plans for the year ahead, proposed activity for future years and is formally agreed and signed off (and regularly reviewed) by senior staff and stakeholders. Appendices to the document may include annual budgets, related key performance indicators, as well as recruitment, retention and engagement campaign schedules.

Membership survey – see also Surveys

Membership surveys are conducted in order to gain a snapshot of general thoughts, feelings and opinions on membership-related activity. Most organisations conduct surveys online and on an annual basis. Research areas vary between organisations, however topic areas are likely to include opinion on the value of current and proposed future member benefits, rating organisational effectiveness, measuring engagement levels and requesting ideas for future policy, lobbying areas, discussion topics.

Memorandum and Articles of Association – see also MemArts and Constitution

Memorandum of understanding (MoU)
A formal agreement between two or more parties, either on a single or a range of issues. Companies and organisations can use MOUs to establish official partnerships. MOUs are not legally binding but they carry a degree of seriousness and mutual respect.

Mentoring – see also Coaching and Peer support
Originally used to describe a sustained relationship between an experienced person and someone who is in the initial stages of their development. The word has now become synonymous with the idea of a trusted adviser – a friend, teacher or wise person. The Oxford English Dictionary defines a mentor as an 'experienced and trusted adviser'. See www.theprofessionalismgroup.co.uk for further information.

Mentoring schemes – see also Peer groups
Schemes that enable the facilitation of mentoring relationships between members. Many professional associations and membership organisations offering such schemes generally provide an online service that enables potential mentors and mentees to express an interest and be identified via the organisation's website. The degree of involvement in the mentor/mentee relationship varies between organisations. Some involve local branches or sections to release pressures on HQ and match mentors with mentees locally.

Merger – see also Acquisition

Mergers between two or more distinct associations or membership organisations usually occur when bringing the two organisations together will offer a solution to sustaining membership growth, address declines and/or combine competence to develop the new organisation further.

Messaging

Effective production and sending out of clear and consistent information, probably via several formats, is important for the organisation to clearly and concisely communicate current and future activities and advice to members.

Methodology

A documented process for the management of activities containing procedures, definition of terms and roles and responsibilities.

Micro-management

A management style whereby a manager closely observes or controls the work of subordinates or employees with excessive attention to minor detail. It is not considered to be a good or effective management style as it can result in very unhappy and demotivated employees.

Milestone

A milestone is a scheduled event signifying the completion of a major deliverable or a set of related deliverables. There is no work associated with a milestone. It is a flag in the work plan to signify some other work has been completed. Usually a milestone is used as a Project checkpoint to validate how the project is progressing and revalidate the remaining work. Milestones are also used in high-level snapshots for management to validate the progress of the project. In many cases there is a decision to be made at the time a milestone is reached.

Mindfulness – see also Zen

"Mindfulness means paying attention in a particular way, on purpose, in the present moment, and non-judgmentally" (Kabat-Zinn). Often described as applied meditation, it involves a conscious direction of our awareness on the emotions, thoughts and sensations occurring in the present moment. Now being applied in the workplace to assist employees to be more effective and to achieve more on a regular basis.

Mind maps

Mind mapping is a simple technique for drawing information in diagram form, instead of writing it in sentences or compiling lists. The diagrams always take the same basic format of a tree, with a single starting point in the middle that branches out, and divides again and again. The tree is made up of words, images or short sentences connected by lines. The display makes it easy for the brain to assimilate large quantities of information while, at the same time, demonstrating potentially unseen linkages between elements of the information included. A very useful tool for Strategic planning, Brainstorming and organisational purposes, as well as planning and conducting meetings etc.

Minimum staffing level (MSL)

In some professions, minimum staffing levels are mandated as the number of staff required to ensure that the job is carried out adequately and without jeopardising safety requirements.

Minutes – see Meeting minutes

Mission statement – see also Vision, Values and Objects

A written declaration of an organisation's core purpose and focus that normally remains unchanged over time. Properly crafted mission statements (1) serve as filters to separate what is important from what is not, (2) clearly state which markets will be served and how, and (3) communicate a sense of intended direction to the entire organisation.
A mission is different from a vision in that the former is the cause and the latter is the effect; a mission is something to be

accomplished whereas a vision is something to be pursued for that accomplishment.

Mistake proofing – see also Proofing process

The use of any device or method that either makes it impossible for an error to occur or makes the error immediately obvious once it has occurred. Usually associated with checking for written or text errors in documents or online environments. Also an essential part of the construction of any process or procedure in order to ensure that errors should not occur during their execution.

Mitigation

The process of taking action to counter the effect of Threats (see entry).

mLearning or Mobile learning

Any sort of learning that happens when the learner is not at a fixed, predetermined location, or learning that happens when the learner takes advantage of the learning opportunities offered by mobile technologies. In other words, with the use of mobile devices, learners can learn anywhere and at any time.

Mobile web

A growing trend that refers to users wirelessly accessing the Internet and web-based applications through a mobile device, such as a smartphone or a tablet. Users tend to access it while on the go and therefore want immediate access to information, such as email, social networking sites or shopping for products.

Model

(a) a person who serves as a target subject for a learner to emulate
(b) a representation of a process or system which show the most important variables in the system in such a way that analysis of the model leads to insights into the system.

Modulus checking

A mathematical term relating to the effective operation of computer systems. Organisations may use modulus checking with their membership databases to check the accuracy of addresses or bank details. Usually this functionality is provided by third party organisations and an annual subscription fee applies.

Monitoring

The capture, analysis and reporting of progress information.

MOOC

Massive Open Online Courses - learning platforms which contain large numbers of online courses delivered over the internet which are generally free of charge. In the UK The Open University is leading development with their FutureLearn platform (www.futurelearn.com). Current market leaders include Udacity, edX and Coursera. Courses typically entail a few hours study per week over a period of six to ten weeks. Many consider that MOOCs will change the face of learning and are an example of disruptive innovation which could pose a threat to membership associations and professional bodies as they offer a new way of learning. However, they also pose many opportunities for collaboration and innovation.

MoSCoW Rules

An acronym for a form of Pioritisation (see entry) that classifies objectives as "Must Have", "Should Have", "Could Have" and "Would like to Have".

Motivation

The combination of a person's desire and energy directed at achieving a goal. It is usually the pre-requisite cause of action.

MSL – see Minimum staffing level

Multi-platform marketing

Engaging with your customers over multiple online and social platforms simultaneously.

MVP – see Member value proposition

Mystery shopping

The use of trained or briefed individuals to experience and measure compliance or any customer service process, by acting as potential customers and in some way reporting back on their experiences in a detailed and objective way. Above all a tool to assess the quality of service, organisation and management, rather than a market research technique. Mystery shopping generally reviews how staff perform against pre-determined standards during an interaction where the staff are engaged.

N

National occupational standards (NOS)

NOS specify the UK standards of performance that people are expected to achieve in their work, and the knowledge and skills they need in order to perform effectively. NOS, which are approved by UK government regulators, are available for almost every role in every sector in the UK.

National vocational qualification (NVQ)

UK qualifications based on demonstrable evidence of competence. The qualifications do not involve any exams. Instead candidates produce a Portfolio (see entry) of documentary evidence which shows that they have competently performed various elements of the syllabus. They are checked by an Independent assessor (see entry) who evaluates them against the competence standard for that subject.

NED – see Non-executive director or (NXD)

Negotiation and influencing

Ways in which to get other people to see things slightly differently or to get them to do something you need them to by utilising interpersonal and communication skills in order to get other people to want to give you their support. Negotiation is a tool that assists parties to obtain an agreement based on their interests, but ultimately, what we do when we negotiate is to attempt to influence others to accept our way. Negotiation is measured by two criteria: Results and effects on relationships. A successful negotiation happens when we achieve our objectives in terms of results and keep the relationship, at least, within cooperative limits.

Network membership scheme

This type of scheme is linked to the requirement for individuals and organisations to network for mutual benefit. Two models are prominent – free membership with pay-to-attend networking events or paid-for membership with reduced cost or free attendance at events.

Networking

Interacting with fellow members to exchange information and develop professional and social contacts.

New product development

The complete development process for bringing a new product or service to market.

Newsletters - see also e-newsletters

A regular publication generally focusing on association or membership organisation activity, progress and/or member focused development. Many organisations are moving from hard copy to electronic and are sending out via professional Email marketing tools which enable self-service design and analytics.

NGO – Non-governmental organisation

A term widely used in the international development field which refers to voluntary or charitable organisations.

Nominations committee

A committee which operates within the organisation's corporate governance structure and performs several duties. These may include the evaluation of the performance of the members of the board, the nomination of candidates to the board and its sub-committees and to ensure the full skillset is met and, often, the hiring and oversight of the performance of the Chief Executive Officer.

Non-executive director (NED) or (NXD)

A director who is a member of the organisation's Board but who does not form part of the Senior management team. They are not employees or affiliated with the organisation in any other way. They should constructively challenge and contribute to the development of strategy, are involved in and monitor the executive activity but are not involved in the day-to-day running of the organisation.

Non-member
An individual who is not yet or is no longer a current member.

Non-member research
Research conducted with individuals who are not yet or are no longer current members. Usually this work is conducted to understand why individuals are not members and what change or development is required in order for them to consider joining or returning to membership. Prominent research methods include online surveys, focus groups and interviews.

Non-verifiable CPD - see also Continuing professional development
This is the term given to learning that cannot be easily measured, e.g. reading a book or watching a video. Many professional associations and membership organisations specify a certain amount that can be undertaken (normally in hours) per year, however this is supported by elements of Verifiable CPD requirement (see entry).

Non-voting members
Some members may not have the right to vote in Council or Committee elections and these members are referred to as non-voting members.

NOS - see National occupational standards

NVQ – see National vocational qualification

NXD – see Non-executive director (NED)

O

Objectives
> A specific outcome that a person, system or organisation aims to achieve within a timeframe and within available resources.

Objects – see also Mission statement, Values and Vision
> The stated, measurable targets of how to achieve the organisation's aims.

Officers
> The group of most senior individuals in specified roles on the Board or Council responsible for an organisation's overall performance. They are held responsible for the success or failure of the organisation.

OMVP (Online member value proposition) – see also Member value proposition
> The degree of value a member places or derives from online member benefits and services.

One-page business plan
> Also known as a one-pager. The detail of the organisation's business plan is deliberately compressed onto a single side of paper in order to make the essential points of the plan more visible.

One-to-one meetings
> An important tool for any manager. One-to-one meetings between the direct report and their manager provide an uninterrupted private time to receive and discuss the employee's status while at the same time providing a vehicle for personalised feedback and mentoring. The time is focused on meeting the individual needs of the employee while at the same time providing timely and accurate status checks for the manager. They are often used during the appraisal process but can be of significant value at all times. One-to-one meetings

between colleagues will also be very valuable.

Online CPD - see also Continuing professional development
Not to be confused with eLearning, online CPD is the ability to log and measure CPD opportunities and activities (online and offline). Online CPD tools are used for this process.

Online event registrations
The facility to offer registration and, in some cases, payment for member events, both live and online, via an event booking facility on the organisation's website.

Online joiner
The term given to individuals who join or apply to join online usually via submission of an online application form.

Online joining
The ability for non-members to join a membership organisation or association online. Typical functionality includes an online form that requires individuals or organisations to submit information (e.g personal/professional details) and make an online subscription payment. Automated welcome emails (including e-receipts) are usually generated on successful online submission. Some organisations enable the online set-up of recurring opt-out payments and this can improve member retention rates.

Online learning – see also e-Learning and Blended learning
Sometimes referred to as eLearning, the ability to learn via the web, the content for which is provided via Online learning environments (OLE) and portals.

Online learning environments (OLE) – see also eLearning
A system for delivering learning materials to students via the web. These systems usually include assessment, student tracking, collaboration and communication tools. They can be accessed remotely, enabling use of mobile devices and at times convenient to the learner. Not just used for delivery of

traditional training subjects but also, increasingly, being used by companies and organisations to deliver staff training.

Online member value proposition – see OMVP

Online payments – see also Direct Debit payments
Payments made via the web. These can include credit card, Direct Debit (UK) and online payment solution providers (e.g. PayPal, WorldPay).

Online renewals
The process of renewing membership via the web.

Online surveys – see also Surveys and Membership surveys
Surveys delivered and completed via the web (e.g. via tools such as Survey Monkey).

Online voting - see Elections and Voting

Open rate - see also e-newsletters, Click-through rate and Mailing house
A measure used as an indication of how many people have viewed or opened an e-mail sent out. It is most commonly expressed as a percentage and calculated by dividing the number of email messages opened by the total number of email messages sent (excluding those that bounced – see Bounced email).

Operations
Jobs or tasks consisting of one or more elements or subtasks, performed typically in one location. Operations transform resources or data inputs into desired services or goods and create and deliver value to members. Two or more connected operations constitute a process. In membership organisations and associations the term will cover all elements of administration relating to the work of the organisation. Operations should be controlled by the Chief Executive and his team.

Operations plan / Operating plan

A short or long-term, highly detailed plan formulated by management to achieve tactical and financial objectives while remaining within resource capacity.

Opt in

Express permission by a member or customer, or a recipient of a mailing, email, or other direct message to allow an organisation to send merchandise, information, or further messages. This is the method generally used by most direct marketing firms, subscription or non-subscription periodicals, information suppliers, etc. After the opt in, the marketer will keep on sending material or messages until the recipient chooses to opt out.

Opt out

Express instruction by a member or customer, or a recipient of a mailing, email, or other direct delivery to stop an organisation from sending merchandise, information or more messages. Responsible online marketers include opt out instructions in their messages or at their sites.

Optimisation

Achieving the best possible solution to a problem in terms of a specified objective function.

Opt-out payment methods

A method of payment that requires the payee (member or non-member) to opt out in order not to pay, e.g. recurring credit card payments or Direct Debit (UK).

Organisation membership

A grade of membership in which membership is granted to an entire organisation or company and benefits are usually applied to the organisation as a whole as well as its staff.

Organisational change – see also Change management

A structured approach in an organisation for ensuring that

changes are smoothly and successfully implemented to achieve lasting benefits.

Organisational culture – see also Culture

Organisational culture is a system of shared values, assumptions, beliefs and norms that unite the staff of the organisation or contribute to its problems. Culture represents the shared expectations and self-image of the organisation. The mature values that create 'tradition', the 'feel' of the organisation over time and the deep, unwritten code that frames 'how we do things around here' all contribute to the culture. Changing or creating cultures can be incredibly difficult.

Organisational maturity (Maturity)

All organisations evolve through a series of development stages, from the point at which they are founded to the time when they have outlived their relevance or usefulness and are wound up. These stages include improving, stable, mature, stale or tired and will affect decisions about future strategy. See www.theprofessionalismgroup.co.uk.

Orientation – see also Induction

Initial induction of new employees into organisations. Objectives include developing employee commitment, easing anxiety, promoting organisational expectations and explaining what the employee can gain from working with the organisation. An especially important process if an individual has no prior experience of the membership sector as working practices are unique compared with other sectors.

Outcomes

The end state or result that is being sought by a programme, organisation, policy or other intervention.

Outputs

Defined as something which is being produced, delivered, broadcast or in some way supplied.

Outsourcing

The contracting out of a business process to a third-party. Also used to describe the practice of handing over control of public services to for-profit corporations.

Overheads

The general, fixed cost of running a business, e.g. rent costs of premises, lighting, and heating expenses, which cannot be charged or attributed to a specific product or part of the work operation and do not vary with output.

P

Panel – see also Committee

A deliberative assembly of members or other stakeholders that ordinarily meets on a regular basis and remains the subordinate to a more senior authority (e.g. the Board of trustees or Council).

Pareto principle

The Pareto principle is often used as an informal gauge in identifying what contribution the individual components of a system make to the whole. Also known as the 80/20 rule as it often reveals that 80% of the effect is created by only 20% of causes.

Partnership

A form of governance structure in which two or more organisations pool money, skills and other resources and share results, profit and loss in accordance with the terms of the partnership agreement.

Pay-as-you-go membership scheme

This model is based on payment for products and services as and when used or required and sometimes adds a premium to the amount charged for services compared to inclusive membership schemes, e.g. conference tickets.

Payment by results (PbR)

A contracting arrangement whereby a provider is only paid in full if they achieve pre-agreed outcomes of their contract. This usually yields greater profit but carries greater risk. In most cases, only part of a contract is subject to PbR.

Payment options

The available payment options for membership and product or service purchases. Common options include credit card, Direct Debit and cheque with a number of organisations now offering online payment options (e.g. through PayPal or WorldPay).

Peak – see Annual hump

Peer groups – see also Mentoring schemes
A peer group can be both a social group and a primary group of people who have similar interests, e.g. career stage, age, background or social status. The members of this group are likely to influence beliefs and behaviours of others in the group. Peer groups often contain hierarchies and distinct patterns of behaviour.

Peer review
Peer review is the evaluation of work by one or more people of similar competence to the producers of the work (peers). It constitutes a form of self-regulation by qualified members of a profession within the relevant field. Peer review methods are employed to maintain standards of quality, improve performance, and provide credibility. In academia peer review is often used to determine the suitability of an academic paper for publication.

Peer support – see also Mentoring and Coaching
A system of giving and receiving help founded on key principles of respect, shared responsibility, and mutual agreement of what is helpful.

Performance appraisal (Performance review, Performance evaluation)
- see also Appraisal process
A method by which the job performance of an employee is evaluated. Performance appraisals are an essential component of career development and consist of regular reviews of employee performance within organisations.

Performance management
Performance management can be regarded as a systematic process by which the overall performance of an organisation can be improved by improving the performance of individuals

within a team framework. It is a means for promoting superior performance by communicating expectations, defining roles within a required competence framework and establishing achievable benchmarks.

Performance standard
A criterion or benchmark against which actual performance is measured.

Performing rights – see also IPR
The right to perform music in public or public places. It is part of copyright law and demands payment to the music's composer/lyricist and publisher (with the royalties generally split 50/50 between the two). Performances are considered "public" if they take place in a public place and the audience is outside of a normal circle of friends and family, including concerts, nightclubs, restaurants, etc. Public performance also includes broadcast and cable television, radio and any other transmitted performance of a live song. Permission to publicly perform or play music must be obtained from the copyright holder or a collective rights organisation prior to performance with licences from both PRS (Performing Rights Society) and PPL (Phonographic Performance Limited).

Personal identification number (PIN)
A number allocated to an individual and used to validate electronic and online transactions.

Personalisation
The provision and alignment of content, both online and offline, that is based on member or user attributes, e.g. location, career stage or membership grade.

PEST or PESTLE analysis – see also SWOT analysis and STEER analysis
Political, Economic, Social and Technological analysis. Used for external analysis when conducting a strategic analysis or carrying out market research, providing an overview of the different macro-environmental factors that the company has

to take into consideration. Some add Legal and Environmental factors to expand the mnemonic to PESTEL or PESTLE. It is a useful strategic tool for understanding market growth or decline, business position, potential and direction for operations. The growing importance of environmental or ecological factors in the first decade of the 21st century have given rise to green business considerations and encouraged widespread use of an updated version of the PEST framework. STEER analysis systematically considers Socio-cultural, Technological, Economic, Ecological, and Regulatory factors.

Plan B

A strategy or plan to be implemented if the original one proves impracticable or unsuccessful. Should always be thought through in advance, preferably while the first choice 'Plan A' is being considered.

Plan-do-check-action (PDCA)

A four step process for quality improvement, sometimes referred to as the Shewhart Cycle (named after the inventor Walter A Shewhart):
- Plan – A plan to effect improvement is developed
- Do – The plan is carried out, on a small scale first if possible
- Check – The effects of the plan are observed
- Action – The results are studied and observed to determine what was learned and what can be predicted.

Planning

A detailed method of examining possibilities for action or direction, then choosing specific steps and stages to achieve the chosen action or direction. Planning allows an organisation to become aware of future needs, opportunities and trends and to avoid dangers and difficulties in achieving the purpose and goals of the organisation.

Policy / Policy development / Policy making

A statement of principles or standards or conduct which guide any decision making in relation to processes, activities and initiatives which happen, or are expected to happen, frequently.

Properly developed and communicated, policies ensure a consistent approach and value to all frequent processes, activities and initiatives. Most importantly, policies must reflect the philosophy and purpose of the organisation.

The process of policy development is almost as important as the policies themselves. Being such an important part of an organisation's governance, management and operation, policy development should be closely linked with improved work practices.

Portfolio/ Career portfolio

Hard copy or online accumulations of evidence which serve as proof of an individual's skills, abilities and potential. They will contain both personal and career critical information.

Positioning

A marketing strategy that aims to make a Brand occupy a distinct position, relative to competing brands, in the mind of the customer.

Post implementation review - see Lessons learned

Post-nominal letters – see also Designatory letters

These are letters placed after the name of a person to indicate that the individual holds a position, educational degree, accreditation, office or honour. An individual may use several different sets of post-nominal letters. The order in which these are listed after a name is based on the order of precedence and category of the order.

Practice

A usual or customary action, the way in which something is actually happening or being done. Quite often the practice differs from the written policy. This may be the result of ignorance, lack of skill or understanding, lack of commitment, a simple slip in standards or, at worst, a determined effort to render the written Policies (see entry) and Procedures (see entry) ineffective. Care should be taken that practices are aligned with policies and procedures, a major requirement in Accreditation (see entry), Performance (see entry), Quality (see entry) or Risk audits (see entry).

Premium membership model

A membership model in which a premium product or benefit elevates the case for membership. As an example, a membership organisation or professional association may be awarded the sole license to deliver government endorsed training in a particular topic area or skill. If this training is not available elsewhere (and is not easily copied) it becomes a premium service and a potential Unique selling point (USP) for the organisation. This in turn can be used to directly leverage membership value and fees, and should contribute towards healthy member recruitment and retention if delivered effectively.

Pre-qualification questionnaire (PQQ)

This common commissioning term defines the process by which interested organisations complete a detailed form, set against the criteria of the contract, which establishes whether they are suitable to enter the full competition. Often undertaken as a tendering process, this filters out unsuitable organisations, saving all parties time and effort.

President / Vice-president

The highest positions in an association or memberhip organisation, often an advocate's role. In professional associations and membership organisations these roles are voluntary and usually held by individuals who have been involved with the organisation for many years.

Press release – see also Public relations (PR)

A written or recorded communication directed at the news media for the purpose of announcing something ostensibly newsworthy. Typically, they are sent to editors and journalists at newspapers, magazines, online broadcast and listing sites, radio stations, television stations or television networks.

Pricing strategies
Associations and membership organisations need to ensure effective pricing strategies are in place. Usually these strategies need to maintain member value, e.g. members will expect to see non-members paying more for products and services.

Primary research - see also Desk research
New research carried out to answer specific issues or questions, acquiring data first hand rather than being gathered from published sources. It can involve questionnaires, surveys or interviews with individuals or small groups. Compare with Secondary or Desk research which makes use of information previously researched for other purposes and publicly available.

Prioritisation
An essential part of any planning process, deciding which of several tasks must be performed or achieved in which order. Some tasks may be resource–dependent or time critical.

Privacy issues
Privacy concerns exist wherever personally identifiable information or other sensitive information is collected and stored – in digital form or otherwise. Improper or non-existent disclosure control can be the root cause for privacy issues.

Privy Council – see also Chartered Institute and Royal Charter
The Privy Council is a formal body of advisers to the Sovereign in the United Kingdom. Its membership is mostly made up of senior politicians who are (or have been) members of either the House of Commons or the House of Lords. The Sovereign issues Royal Charters, on the advice of the Privy Council, which grant special status to incorporated bodies. They are used to grant chartered status to certain professional or educational bodies on application.

Probability
Usually used in the context of Risk as a measure of the chance that a risk event may occur.

Procedure / Procedures manual

Detailed implementation guidelines, methods or instructions to be followed in specific circumstances, setting out who does what, in what manner and in what sequence. Procedures can be either mandatory or discretionary.

Process

A series of actions which produce a change or development: the 'how' of governance, management and operation.

Process improvement

Activities designed to identify and eliminate causes of poor quality, process variation and non-value added activities.

Product analysis

Studying how well a product or service does its job by questioning a number of issues including function and purpose, how various components work together, who would buy it, whether it is unique and how well it does its job compared to other similar products or services.

Product life cycle

A business analysis that attempts to identify a set of common stages in the life of commercial products used to map the lifespan of the product, i.e. the stages through which a product goes during its lifespan; for example, introduction, promotion, growth, maturity and decline.

Product / Service oriented membership model

An emerging model in which membership may form a secondary value-added and inclusive benefit of purchasing a particular product or service.

Productivity

An overall measure of the ability to produce a product or service. It is the actual output of production compared to the actual input of resources.

Professional body

A professional body comprises individuals in a particular sector or profession within which training and education are a primary feature alongside activities such as lobbying and representation. Some professional bodies regulate their industries, with individuals needing the appropriate qualifications to practice and are subject to Disciplinary procedures (see entry) if they do not perform to agreed standards.

Professional development

Refers to the acquisition of skills and knowledge, both for personal and career development. Professional development encompasses all types of facilitated learning opportunities, ranging from college degrees to formal coursework, conferences and informal learning opportunities in the workplace.

Professional services

Occupations in the third sector requiring special training, some of which require practitioners to hold professional qualifications or licenses.

Professional standards

Professional standards set the minimum requirement for practice and conduct in various professions and work sectors.

Professionalism

The combination of skills, attitudes and character attributes which ensure that an individual inspires trust and confidence in those around them. Professionalism applies to both individuals and to the organisations in which they work. For further information see "Professionalism – the ABC for Success" by Susie Kay, published by Professionalism Books (see end pages), and www.theprofessionalismgroup.co.uk.

Profile

Representation of user constructed with varying amounts of personally identifying information, e.g. online profile

Profit and loss forecast (P&L)

A projection of how much money could be brought in by selling products or services and how much profit will be made from these sales. In good times, it is used to ensure that there will be enough money coming in to exceed the costs of providing goods and services in order to deliver a solid profit. In tough times, P&L can play an essential role in showing what kind of a plan is needed to return to breakeven, ensuring survival until better times arrive.

Pro-forma invoice

A document that states a commitment on part of the seller to deliver the products or services as notified to the buyer for a specific price. It is not a true invoice.

Programme management – see also Project management

The management and oversight of a significant long-term activity, often composed of several projects, as opposed to a unique project. It is normally defined as a line item in the organisation's strategy and budget

Project life cycle

The phases through which most projects pass from initial idea, through all phases to closure.

Project management – see also Programme management

Project management is the application of processes, methods, knowledge, skills and experience to achieve project objectives. A project is a unique, transient endeavour, undertaken to achieve planned objectives, which could be defined in terms of outputs, outcomes or benefits. A project is usually deemed to be a success if it achieves the objectives according to their acceptance criteria, within an agreed timescale and budget (Association for Project Management).

Project management triangle - see also Time/Cost/Quality triangle

Illustrated by the saying: "You can have it good, fast, or cheap. Pick two." Every project balances a "triangle" of time, money, and scope — you can't change one without affecting at least one of the others. The project manager's job is to keep the whole triangle from falling apart.

Project scope – see also Scope creep

The scope of a project is the sum total of all project products and their requirements or features. Sometimes scope is used to refer to the totality of work needed to complete a project.

Proofing process – see also Mistake proofing

Also known as mistake proofing. The use of any device or method that either makes it unlikely for an error to occur or makes the error immediately obvious once it has occurred. Usually associated with checking for written or text errors in documents or online environments. Also an essential part of the construction of any process or procedure in order to ensure that errors should not occur during their execution.

Property asset management - see Facilities management

Proposal

Solicited or unsolicited submission by one party to supply or buy certain goods or services from another. Unlike an offer, a proposal is not a promise or commitment but, if accepted by the other party, its proposer is expected to follow through and negotiate for the creation of a binding contract. If submitted in response to a request for proposals then it normally constitutes a bid.

Protocol

The purpose of protocols is to ensure a consistent quality and standard of procedure, so that a consistent and replicable quality of service delivery can be delivered. Protocol agreements are a quality tool. Protocols explain the agreement upon which the delivery of particular services will be provided by Organisation A to Organisation B, or to the clients / service-users / customers of Organisation B.

Proxy voting - see also Elections

A form of voting whereby members may delegate their voting power to other members to vote in their absence.

Provisional member

An individual who is pursuing the entry requirements to enable them to secure membership.

Psychometric tests

A set of tests generally used to discover how good someone is at a particular skill, such as verbal or numerical reasoning. This is different to the related area of psychometric profiling which is used to build a picture of either an individual or a team, such as identifying their values, personality type or occupational interests.

Public Benefit

A critical term not clearly defined in the Charities Act 2011. In England and Wales, public benefit is part of what it means to be a charity so any organisation purporting to have charitable Objects must answer both the 'public' and 'benefit' requirement test. The organisation must be set up and run with purposes which are exclusively charitable for the public benefit and report on this in the Annual report.

Public relations (PR) – see also Press Release

Public Relations is the discipline which looks after reputation, with the aim of earning understanding and support and influencing opinion and behaviour. It is the planned and sustained effort to establish and maintain goodwill and mutual understanding between an organisation and its publics (Chartered Institute of Public Relations).

Publications – see also Magazines and Journals

Many associations and membership organisations publish content in the form of inclusive or paid-for books, ebooks, journals and/or e-journals.

Publisher membership model

A membership model in which organisations place emphasis on the print or digital journal/magazine. Primary research indicates the prevailing use of the word subscriber rather than member and unsurprisingly this model is used by a number of leading publishers. A great example is the National Geographic website. Supplementary online benefits include member-area access (for digital downloads) and exclusive offers and discounts.

Q

QA (Quality Assurance)

A system for ensuring a desired level of quality in the development, production or delivery of products and services.

Qualification – see also Certification

Professional qualifications in the United Kingdom are generally awarded by professional bodies, often in line with their Charters. These qualifications are subject to the European directives on professional qualifications. Many, but not all, professional qualifications are 'Chartered' qualifications, and follow on from having achieved an academic qualification at degree level (or having an equivalent qualification or experiential evidence). They are mainly subject to CPD verification and adherence to Professional standards.

Qualitative research – see also Research

A method of inquiry employed in many different academic disciplines, traditionally in the social sciences, but also in market research and further contexts. Qualitative researchers aim to gather an in-depth understanding of human behaviour and the reasons that govern such behaviour. The qualitative method investigates the why and how of decision making, not just what, where, when. Hence, smaller but focused samples are more often used than large samples

Quality assurance – see QA

Quantifying

To determine or measure the quantity of something or expressing the value of something in numerical form.

Quantitative research – see also Research

Quantitative research refers to the systematic empirical investigation of social phenomena via statistical, mathematical or numerical data or computational techniques.

Quorate

In order for a committee/board meeting/AGM/EGM to make formal decisions there is a requirement that a minimum number of committee members are present. The relevant minimum number will usually be defined in the MemArts (Memorandum and Articles of Association – see entry) or Terms of Reference (see entry) for each body.

Quorum

The minimum number of officers and members of a committee or organisation, usually a majority, who must be present for valid transaction of business. The minimum number acceptable is usually defined in the Terms of Reference for that body.

R

RAG reports – see also Risk / Risk assessment and Risk register
Used as a dashboard reporting system. RAG is an acronym for
Red, Amber, Green and is a form of report where measurable
information is classified by colour in the manner of a traffic light
system. For each colour there is a pre-determined action which
usually constitutes escalation to a higher level of management
and, as such, is a form of trigger mechanism.

RASCI definitions
A responsibility assignment matrix which describes the
participation by various roles in completing tasks or deliverables
for a project or business process:

Responsible: the person who is owner of the element of work
Accountable: the person to whom "R - responsible" is
Accountable and is the authority who has final approval
Supportive: person who provides resources or plays a
supporting role
Consulted: person who provides information and/or expertise
necessary to complete the work.

Rationale
Explanation of the logical reasons or principles employed in
consciously arriving at a decision or estimate. Rationales usually
document why a particular choice was made, how the basis
of its selection was developed, why and how the particular
information or assumptions were relied on and why the
conclusion is deemed credible or realistic.

Reconfiguration
In this context usually to change the shape or formation of
membership grades.

Reciprocal agreement
A duty owed by one individual to another and vice versa. It is a

type of agreement that bears upon or binds two parties in an equal manner. Also known as a reciprocal obligation.

Record(s) management

This term usually refers to the management of member records and historic governance related documents including copies of Agendas and Minutes (hard copy and electronic).

Record management system (RMS)

A system used to store records either electronically or in hard copy.

Recruitment – see Member recruitment

Regional network

Many membership organisations and associations have regional structures that together form a national network.

Regional structure - see also Branch structure and Chapters

The structure of regional activity or the organisation's presence within the region, e.g. each region may have an executive committee formed of members, usually acting in a volunteer capacity. Roles may include Chair, Treasurer and Secretary.

Registrar

An official responsible for keeping a register or official records.

Regulations

A set of laws, rules or orders prescribed by an authority, usually a Regulatory body, to regulate or control a set of behaviours, an activity or an organisation.

Regulatory body - see also Enforcement / Enforcement bodies

A regulatory body (or regulatory authority, regulatory agency or regulator) is a body formed or mandated under the terms of a legislative act or statute to ensure compliance with the provisions of the act, and in carrying out its purpose. An independent regulatory agency is independent from other branches or arms of government. Some independent regulatory agencies perform investigations or audits and some are authorised to impose fines on relevant parties and order certain measures when shortcomings are established beyond question.

Re-instatement

This term refers to the re-instatement of an individual or organisation back into membership, usually following non-payment of fees or suspension of membership.

Rejoiner campaign

A membership focused campaign targeted at individuals or organisations who were previously in membership.

Relationship management

The management of relationships by the organisation with key stakeholders, e.g. members, officers, government and the general public.

Reminder letter

These are typically sent following non-renewal by the membership renewal date. Various reminder letters are sent before the membership is lapsed.

Remote working – see also Home working

Home workers are defined by the International Labour Organisation as people working from their homes or from other premises of their choosing other than the workplace, for payment, which results in a product or service specified by the employer. Recently, the phenomenon of home working has grown with increased use of communication technology.

Removal – see Member removal and Strike off

Remuneration committee

A committee responsible for guiding policy on the remuneration of staff, officers and other stakeholders. They must also ensure that arrangements support the strategic aims of the organisation and enable recruitment, motivation and retention while also complying with the requirements of regulation.

Renewals

The process of enabling and managing membership year on year.

Renewal date

The date by which membership should be renewed. Usually a short grace period is given following non-payment by this date.

Renewal form

The form used to renew membership (often sent in annual renewals mailings along with a covering letter, payment form and pre-paid envelope. A growing number of organisations pre-populate this form and many are moving to online renewals forms and processes.

Renewal period

The period within which members are invited to renew their annual membership.

Renewal rate

The renewal rate is ordinarily the percentage of members who renew their annual membership subscription.

Renewal schedule

Most professional associations and membership organisations have a formal renewal schedule in place which ensures that the organisation is sending out invitations to renew at the appropriate time of year.

Note: The MemberWise Network investigates optimal unequal schedules in the Perfect Membership Guide advice sheet.

Re-organisation

In a similar way to other types of organisations, associations and membership organisations need to evolve. Over recent years (particularly due to the economic downturn) more emphasis has been placed on this activity along with restructuring and focusing on web/online self-service based tools and resources.

Reporting and analytics – see also Analytics

Analytics is the discovery and communication of meaningful patterns in data. Key examples of the usage of this word within the membership and association sector include web analytics and membership survey analytics. Reporting of the data and derived conclusions encourage more informed strategic debate and future direction.

Representative body

A senior committee deemed to be representative (of a trade or profession) and sometimes responsible for policy and governance related direction, development and change.

Research – see also Qualitative research and Quantitative research

Membership organisations and associations conduct research to poll opinion and establish a deeper understanding on particular topics. A growing number of organisations conduct an annual online Membership survey that covers a range of topic areas. Effective surveys should establish emerging member needs, trends and feelings on particular topic areas. In response the organisation can then develop outcome focused activities that provide value and enable stronger member engagement. Research is conducted with various groups including members, non-members and other key stakeholder groups.

Reserve(s)

A sum of money or time, set aside to deal with the effects of risk or change during an activity or project. Also a fund of money set aside, and normally untouched during normal operations, which acts as a financial cushion for emergency situations.

Resource

A source from which benefit is produced.

Resource management
> The process of using an organisation's resources in the most efficient way possible. These resources can include tangible resources such as goods and equipment, financial resources and labour resources such as employees.

Responsible – see also RASCI definitions
> The person who is owner of the element of work.

Restricted fund – see also Designated fund
> A reserve of money that can only be used for specific purposes. Restricted funds provide reassurance to donors that their contributions will be used in a manner they have chosen.

Restructuring
> Restructuring tends to refer to the organisational development activity of restructuring staff, teams and departments.

Retention – see Member Retention

Retention rate – see Member Retention Rate

Retired member – see also Life member
> A retired member is one who has retired from the industry or profession but still wishes to remain active within the association in order to network with peers and colleagues or continue to contribute their expertise in some way.

Return on investment (ROI)
> Usually expressed as a percentage, return on investment is a measure of profitability that indicates whether or not an organisation is using its resources in an efficient manner. Usually measured as the ratio of the net income to the average capital employed in a project or in the organisation as a whole.

Returning member
> A previously lapsed or non-renewing member returning to membership.

Revalidation

> Associations and membership organisations (particularly within medicine and Chartered qualifications) may provide support for members who are required by law to revalidate their knowledge and skills. This may be in the form of CPD and other learning opportunities or evidence collection leading to periodic re-assessments (see CPD requirement, ePortfolio and Portfolio).

Revenue stream

> A revenue stream is simply another name for income, but possibly because it sounds more sophisticated than the word sales, was borrowed from investment terminology where assets are said to have a future revenue stream. More specifically, the phrase is often qualified by modifiers such as 'new' or 'additional'. The phrase also comes in handy in the digital age where revenues are sometimes generated in novel ways that do not resemble old-fashioned sales across a counter.

Review

> Membership organisations and associations conduct reviews in order to evaluate a range of areas or topics and to prevent the organisation from becoming stale. Examples include organisational review, function-specific review, departmental review, publication review, product/service review, member benefit review and generational review.

Risk / Risk assessment , Risk audit / Risk management – see also Business continuity planning

> The overall process of managing risk. The process usually comprises five stages starting with risk planning, followed by risk identification and analysis. The next stage is to plan how they should be addressed. Risks will then be listed in a risk log and will be monitored to check for the occurrence of risks. If preventative measures do not work and a risk occurs then a contingency plan may be implemented. Often uses the RAG reporting system (see entry)

Risk averse

> A description of an individual (or organisation) who, when faced

with two potential courses of action with a similar expected return (but different risks), will prefer the one with the lower risk.

Risk avoidance

A risk assessment technique which attempts, pre-activity, to eliminate perceived hazards, actions and exposures which might place an organisation's valuable assets at risk.

Risk log – see Risk register

Risk register

A list of identified risks that will include information such as a description, estimates of impact and probability, owner, proximity, current status, etc. Also known as a risk log. These registers identify and hold information relating to identified risks for a particular purpose, role or project and allow assessment and management of the risks involved. Often uses the RAG reporting system (see entry) to categorise identified risks.

RMS - see Record management system

ROI – see Return on investment

Rolling renewals

This type of membership scheme model enables members to renew on the anniversary of their joining date or month.

Rolling renewals calendar

Rolling renewals enable members to join on a particular date and ordinarily their membership will expire 12 months from joining (unlike fixed renewals which are charged pro-rata). In order for a membership organisation or association to effectively manage this process a rolling renewals calendar enables this activity to be monitored and conducted in a structured and robust manner. Rolling renewals calendars are also likely to include the scheduling of pre-renewal communications, post-renewal communications and communications linked to non-renewal.

Royal Charter - see also Chartered Institute and Privy Council
> A Royal Charter is granted by the sovereign of Great Britain and Northern Ireland on the advice of the Privy Council as a way of incorporating a group into a public or private organisation.

Running costs
> The amount regularly spent to operate an organisation, used for items such as salaries, utilities, building costs, etc.

S

Scenario development / Scenario planning - see also Horizon scanning and PESTLE analysis

> A strategic planning method that explores possible futures. If you are aware of what could happen then you are more likely to be able to deal with what will happen. It involves identifying trends and exploring their implications, probably as high medium and low forecasts. Asks the 'What if?' question and identifies risks.

Schedule / Scheduling

> Determining when an activity or series of activities (as in a project) should start or end. These decisions may be dependent on duration, other activities or dependencies, resource availability and required completion date.

Scope creep – see also Project scope

> The term often used to describe the continual extension of the scope of an activity or project due to poor or inadequate diligence, management or oversight. The problem may occur in project management where the initial objectives of the project are placed in jeopardy by a gradual increase in overall objectives as the project progresses. The requirements of the new objectives can exceed the resources allocated to the project resulting in the project missing deadlines, overrunning budgets or failing completely.

Search engine optimisation (SEO) – see also Website maximisation

> Search engine optimisation (SEO) is the process of affecting the visibility of a website or a web page in a search engine's search results. In general, the earlier (or higher ranked on the search results page), and more frequently a site appears in the search results list, the more visitors it will receive from the search engine's users. As a marketing strategy, SEO considers how search engines work, what people search for, the actual search terms or keywords typed into search engines and which

search engines are preferred by the target audience. Optimising a website may involve editing its content, HTML and associated coding to both increase its relevance to specific keywords and to remove barriers to the indexing activities of search engines. Promoting a site to increase the number of backlinks, or inbound links, is another SEO tactic.

Secondary research – see Desk research

Secretary - see Company Secretary

Secretary General – see also Chief Executive Officer and General Manager
The highest ranking paid management officer in the organisation may be known as the Secretary General, with responsibility for human, financial and technical operations, as well as delivery of the organisation's strategy. Typically the Secretary General (or equivalent) is accountable to the Board of directors (or Board of Trustees). Alternative job titles may include Chief Executive or Director General.

Sections – see also Faculties
Local member activity can be structured into regional branches (e.g. London Branch) and further subdivided, depending on size, into local sections (e.g. South West London Section).

Sector Skills Council (SSC)
Employer-led organisations covering specific industries in the UK, responsible for understanding future skills needs for their sector and contributing to the relevant National Occupational Standards. Their key goals are to support employers in developing and managing apprenticeship standards, to reduce skills gaps and shortages and improve productivity. At time of print there are 19 in existence plus four additional Sector Skills bodies.

Segmentation – see Member segmentation

Self-regulation
When an organisation itself exercises some degree of regulatory authority over an industry or profession. The regulatory authority could be applied in addition to some form of government regulation, or it could fill the vacuum of an absence of government oversight and regulation.

Self-service
Increasingly membership organisations are aspiring to enable members to better self-serve in order to optimise convenience and reduce cost. Great emphasis is now being placed on online self-service functionality and this may include enabling members to select special interest areas, online renewal and online event registration.

Self-study
A form of study in which the individual is, to a large extent, responsible for their own instruction without direct supervision or attendance in a conventional classroom environment.

Senior management team (SMT) – see also Leadership team
A team of individuals at the highest level of the organisation who have the day-to-day responsibilities of managing the organisation.

Sensitive data
Membership organisations and associations hold comparatively high levels of sensitive data and so need to comply with the UK Data Protection Act. Examples of sensitive data may include member data such as birth date, age, address, bank account number, ethnicity, email address.

SEO – see Search engine optimisation

Service level agreement (SLA)
A growing number of membership organisations and professional associations are providing members with service level agreements which specifically outline what a member

can expect in return for their annual membership subscription fee, e.g. telephone support between Monday and Friday with a call waiting period of no longer than 2 minutes. SLAs are also negotiated and agreed with key suppliers (e.g. CRM or database providers) to ensure their product or service provision is fit for purpose.

Service / Product oriented membership model

An emerging membership model focused on a particular product or service.

Service provision

Performing a task for a business or person that wants or requires it in exchange for acceptable compensation.

Service users

People who benefit from a service provided by a third-sector organisation, as distinct from 'customer' which implies that people pay for the services provided.

Shadowing

Spending time with someone who is doing a particular job, either within your own organisation or outside it, in order to learn how to do it or to appreciate its context and complexities.

Showstopper

An issue which has the potential to stop the progress, operation or functioning of some aspect of business or prevent agreement being reached.

SIG - see Special / Specific interest group and Market interest group

A group formed of individuals or organisations with a shared interest in a particular topic area. More specifically within associations and membership organisations it refers to a particular subset of membership who have an interest in common and might well require or welcome specific or unique resources.

Sign-off process
> The process of gaining final agreement and sign-off for a particular task, project or programme from all stakeholders, prior to implementation.

Silent generation – see also Generational differences
> Silent generation is a label for the generation of people born between 1925 and the end of World War II in 1945. The label was originally applied to people in North America but has also been applied to those in Western Europe, Australasia and South America as this was a time of great deprivation and hardship.

Silo working / Silo mentality – see also Matrix working
> An attitude found in some organisations that occurs when departments or groups do not want to share information or work with other individuals, teams or departments within the same organisation. A silo mentality reduces efficiency, fails to acknowledge commercial objectives and can be a contributing factor to a failing corporate culture.

Situational analysis – see also Market audit
> Situation analysis refers to a collection of methods used by managers to analyse an organisation's internal and external environment to understand the organisation's capabilities, customers, and business environment.

Skills
> Skills are described as those abilities which people develop and use with colleagues, ideas or physical objects. Hence they are often classified as interpersonal, cognitive and technical skills.

Skills audit
> A review or assessment process carried out to establish whether an individual or a particular group of individuals can offer the required skills and competences needed to carry out specific tasks or roles. This especially refers to the total skills available within Trustee boards and Committees. The exercise is often carried out to discover whether skills gaps exist which need to

be filled.

SLA – see Service level agreement

Small or medium enterprise (SME)

A small or medium enterprise is a business whose personnel numbers and turnover fall below certain limits. The abbreviation 'SME' is used in the European Union and by international organisations such as the World Bank, United Nations and the World Trade Organisation. Small enterprises, including micro-companies and start-ups, vastly outnumber large companies and employ many more people. SMEs are also said to be responsible for driving innovation and competition in many economic sectors.

SMART objectives

A simple acronym which provides an effective way to set Objectives (see entry). A SMART objective is Specific, Measurable, Achievable, Realistic and Time-scaled. An objective constructed following these rules is more likely to succeed because it provides clear guidance on what is to be achieved and by when.

SME - see Small or medium enterprise

SMT – see Senior management team – see also Leadership team

Social enterprise

An organisation which applies commercial strategies to maximise improvements in human and environmental well-being, rather than maximising profits for external shareholders. Social enterprises can be structured as for-profit or non-profit, and may take the form of a co-operative, mutual organisation, a social business or a charity.

Social media membership scheme

This type of scheme is predominantly offered either free of charge or inclusive as a member benefit to enable members to network online, providing communities of interest. Many organisations offer free access to non-members in order to market membership and capture details for marketing purposes.

Social media strategy –see also LinkedIn and Twitter

The development and deployment of strategic plans for social media activity that consider how social media can be used and if it is needed for social communications internally and externally. The strategy should harness value from collaborative relationships and be used as a tool to manage and monitor brand reputation (internally and externally).

Social networking

The use of websites and applications to interact with others.

Soft skills - see Interpersonal Skills

Special / Specific interest group (SIG) – see SIG

Sponsorship

To sponsor or support an activity, event or organisation financially or through the provision of support, products or services.

Spot purchase

The ad hoc and unsecured purchase of services. This does not bring guaranteed income over a period of time that a contracted purchase may do. As a result does not carry as much risk but does give organisations less security.

SSC - see Sector Skills Council

SSL certificate

Secure socket layer (SSL) is a protocol for encrypting and sending data in a secure manner between two destinations. SSL also plays an important role in validating the identity of websites using certificates. An SSL certificate tells the user that a website is authentic, and that this fact has been validated by a third-party certificate authority.

Staff engagement – see also Employee engagement and Corporate
social responsibility
> The emotional commitment an employee has to the
> organisation and its goals.

Stakeholder(s)
> A person, group or organisation that has an acknowledged
> interest or concern in an organisation. Stakeholders can affect
> or be affected by the organisation's actions, objectives and
> policies.

Standard
> An established norm against which measurements are
> compared, usually formal but can also be informal. Can also be
> defined as the time allowed to perform a task, including the
> quality and quantity of work to be produced.

Start-up costs
> Non-recurring costs associated with setting up an organisation
> or a business, such as accountant's fees, legal fees, registration
> charges, as well as advertising, promotional activities and
> employee training.

Statistics – see also User statistics
> The collection, organisation, analysis, interpretation and
> presentation of data.

Status
> An accepted or official position, especially in a social group;
> position or rank relative to that of others. In relation to
> membership, the term can denote a level of membership or
> whether a member is inactive, etc.

STEER analysis - see also PESTLE analysis and SWOT analysis
> A form of business analysis which looks at Socio-cultural,
> Technological, Economical, Ecological and Regulatory factors

when devising a business strategy plan.

Steering committee

An advisory committee usually made up of high level stakeholders and experts who provide guidance on key issues such as policy and objectives, budgetary control, marketing strategy, resource allocation and decisions involving large expenditures.

Strapline

A strapline is an explanatory phrase which usually follows or is part of a Brand name or the title of an article, e.g. on a rejoiner form the title may clearly state 'Rejoiner Form' at the top of the page but might also include a strapline below which might feature the words 'There has never been a better time to come back to membership'.

Strategic alliance

An agreement for cooperation among two or more organisations to work together toward common objectives. Unlike a Joint venture, organisations in a strategic alliance do not form a new entity to further their aims but collaborate while remaining apart and distinct.

Strategic objective

A broadly defined, usually externally focused, objective that an organisation must achieve to make its strategy succeed.

Strategic plan

A broadly defined plan aimed at creating a desired future.

Strategic planning process

The process of reducing possible alternatives to selected and specific courses of action over a three to five year period, which are most likely to achieve and enrich the purpose for which the organisation exists. Constructing the strategic plan is the responsibility of the senior board of the organisation (Trustee board or Council) and the operational detail is the responsibility of the Chief Executive and his staff team.

Strategy

A method or plan chosen to bring about a desired future, such as achievement of a goal or solution to a problem. The art and science of planning and marshalling resources for their most efficient and effective use.

Straw man

The term refers to a document put out to provoke discussion about the potential flaws and disadvantages of an idea, with the aim of creating solutions and better ideas.

Stress

The real or perceived demand on the mind, emotions, spirit or body. Too much stress puts an undue amount of pressure on us and drives us into a state of tension. Controlled stress – or everyday pressure – can act as a motivator and should not have negative effects. All employers have a duty of care to their employees and have responsibility to ensure that employees are not unduly affected by workplace stress.

Strike-off - see also Member removal and Removal

To remove or erase an individual from a membership list or record.

Student member

A class of membership open only to those individuals who can prove that they are following a course of study at a reputable education establishment.

Subscription fees – see also Tax relief

A payment or arrangement to pay regular instalments for membership of an organisation or some elements of membership, e.g. journals or online resources. In some instances individuals can obtain tax relief on their subscription.

Subsidised membership

A membership subscription fee where part or all of the fee is not charged to the member in order to either make it possible to afford to be in membership or in recognition of meeting some other qualifying condition.

Succession planning

A process for identifying and developing individuals to increase the availability of experienced and capable people ready to replace leaders and those in key positions within an organisation.

Supply chain

Supply chains include every company that comes into contact with a particular product or service. Specifically, the supply chain encompasses the steps it takes to get that product or service from the supplier to the customer. Supply chain management is a crucial process for many companies which strive to have the most optimised supply chain as this usually translates to lower costs for the company. A supply chain is, therefore, a system of organisations, people, activities, information, and resources involved in moving a product or service from supplier to customer and may also include activities if, at any point, there is residual value in recycling after use.

Supportive – see also RASCI definitions

A person who provides resources or plays a supporting role.

Surveys – see also Online surveys and Membership surveys

Sustainability

The quality of not being harmful to the environment or depleting natural resources, and thereby supporting long-term ecological balance. The term is occasionally extended to other resources such as finance and staff time.

SWOT analysis or SWOT Matrix – see also PESTLE analysis and STEER analysis

> A structured planning method used to evaluate the Strengths, Weaknesses, Opportunities, and Threats involved in a project or business venture. A SWOT analysis can be carried out for a product, place, industry or person. It involves specifying the objective of the business venture or project and identifying the internal and external factors that are favourable and unfavourable to achieving that objective.

Synchronous learning – see also Asynchronous learning and eLearning

> This term refers to a learning environment in which everyone takes part at the same time. A lecture is an example of synchronous learning in a face-to-face environment, where learners and teachers are all in the same place at the same time.

Systems

> A set of detailed methods, procedures and routines created to carry out a specific activity, perform a duty or solve a problem. Interrelated and interdependent elements continually influence one another (directly or indirectly) to maintain their activity and the existence of the system, in order to achieve the goal of the system.

T

Tactics
> Means by which a strategy is carried out; planned and ad hoc activities meant to deal with the demands of the moment, and to move from one milestone to other in pursuit of the overall goal(s). In an organisation, strategy is decided by the Board of directors and tactics by the department heads for implementation by staff.

Talking heads
> These usually take the format of published or online video or TV interviews featuring an individual who provides an overview on a particular subject, topic or specialism. These may feature in journals and online and are seen by many as an engaging way to create awareness, e.g. Council members of a professional body could be interviewed in order to promote their particular sector or skill set to university students considering their future career.

Targeting strategy
> The selection of potential members to whom an organisation wishes to sell membership as well as other products and services. The strategy involves segmenting the market, choosing which segments are appropriate and determining the products that will be offered in each segment. Targeting may determine whether a particular segment should receive a generic or customised product, depending on expectations of volume and competition. Also called targeting.

Targets – see also KPI / KPT
> Targets are specific, quantifiable measurements that are critical to the success of a company. They vary between organisations and sectors but should always, if implemented and monitored correctly, help a business define and measure progress toward both short-term and long-term organisational goals.

Task group – see also Working Group

A group of people working together temporarily until a specific goal is achieved and then usually disbanded.

Tax exemptions

A tax exemption is simply an amount of money that's not subject to tax and may be granted to certain organisations, persons, income, property or other normally taxable items.

Taxonomy

The practice and science (study) of classification of things or concepts, plus the principles that underlie such classification.

Tax relief – see also Subscription fees

Amounts, including some subscription fees, which are allowances against an individual's annual personal income tax, thereby reducing the amount of tax paid.

Team building

Team building refers to the various activities undertaken to motivate members of any size team in order to increase the overall performance of the whole team.

Temperature check

A means of regularly checking to ensure that the various operational elements are running smoothly and the organisation's systems are under control.

Tendering process – see Invitation to tender (ITT)

Terms and conditions

A set of rules or legal terms which one must agree to abide by in order to make sales, form a contract or use a service.

Terms of reference

A statement of the background, objectives and purpose of a working group, project or proposal.

Test marketing
> A stage in product development where the product and its marketing plan are exposed to a carefully chosen sample of the population to decide on whether to reject it before a full scale launch.

Testimonial
> A person's written or spoken statement extolling the virtue of an individual, organisation, product or service.

Third party suppliers
> A supplier (or service provider) who is not directly controlled by either the seller (first party) or the customer/buyer (second party) in a business transaction. The third party is considered independent from the other two, even if hired by them, because not all control is vested in that connection.

Third Sector
> The part of an economy or society comprising non-governmental and non-profit-making organisations or associations, including charities, voluntary and community groups, cooperatives, etc.

Thought shower – see also Brainstorming
> The politically correct term thought shower is now also being used to describe the types of activities collectively described as Brainstorming (see entry).

Threats
> A Risk (see entry) which might have a negative impact on an activity or project.

Tiered membership structure
> This type of membership scheme is offered widely within the professional and learned body sector. Recognisable grade names include student, affiliate, associate, member and fellow and acceptance criteria are usually linked to career or knowledge progression.

Time/Cost/Quality triangle - see also Project management triangle
Illustrated by the saying: "You can have it good, fast, or cheap. Pick two." Every project balances a "triangle" of time, money, and scope — you can't change one without affecting at least one of the others. The project manager's job is to keep the whole triangle from falling apart.

Tipping point
Described by social scientist author Malcolm Gladwell as "that magic moment when an idea, trend or social behaviour crosses a threshold, tips and spreads like wildfire".

TOIL (Time off in lieu) - see also Flexitime and Flexible working
Where eligible members of staff have worked agreed additional hours above their normal contracted working week, TOIL is a process by which employees may take time off from work as compensation and in agreement with their line manager.

Total quality management (TQM)
Describes Japanese style management approaches to quality improvement. It includes the long term success of the organisation through customer satisfaction and is based on participation of all members of the organisation in improving process, products, service, culture, etc.

Tracking codes
In the Google Analytics programme, a Tracking Code is a small snippet of code inserted into an HTML page. When the HTML page is loaded, the tracking code contacts the Analytics server and logs a page view for that page, and also captures information about the visit and non-identifying information about the visitor.

Trade association or Trade federation
Representative bodies for groups of companies or other organisations with common interests. Most cover a specific sector or sub-sector of industry, but some cover processes or functions.

Trade exhibition – see Exhibition

Trade journal or Trade magazine

A publication covering, and intended to reach, a specific industry or type of business.

Trading arm / Trading subsidiary

Organisations may set up a subsidiary business or trading arm (in line with their primary mission) as a way to raise funds or generate income on a more substantial or permanent basis. It will be a non-charitable trading company – a private limited company, although they might be set up as a Social enterprise or community business depending on the context and Objects of the organisation.

Trait

A distinguishing quality or characteristic of a person. For a particular trait to be well developed, that person must first believe in and value that trait.

Transparency

Lack of hidden agendas and conditions, accompanied by the availability of full information required for collaboration, cooperation and collective decision making. The minimum degree of disclosure to which agreements, dealings, practices and transactions are open to all for verification. An essential condition for a free and open exchange whereby the rules and reasons behind regulatory measures are fair and clear to all participants.

Treasurer

An Officer appointed to administer or manage the financial assets and liabilities of a membership organisation or professional association. The individual will have a watchdog role over all aspects of financial management, working closely with other members of the Board and Senior management team to safeguard the organisation's finances. It is important to note that although the Treasurer ensures that these responsibilities are met, much of the work may be delegated to a Finance committee and paid staff.

Trial membership

A defined period of time during which an individual may try out some areas of membership to see whether they wish to take up long-term membership.

Triggers / Database triggers

A procedural code within a database which is automatically executed in response to certain events happening, usually when entering new information into the database. The trigger is mostly used for maintaining the integrity of the information on the database or to enhance and streamline the user experience of the member. For example, when a new member record is added this will trigger the production of a welcome letter to be sent to the new member.

Trust

An arrangement, defined by law, where someone or a group of people take on the responsibility for assets for the benefit of another group of people. The people assigned to administer the trust are known as Trustees and those benefiting, the beneficiaries.

Trustee

An individual (usually a current member) who is elected (ordinarily by the membership) to sit on an association or membership organisation's board of trustees.

Trustee board - see also Board member

A trustee board is a body of elected members who jointly oversee the activities of a membership organisation or professional association. Many organisations will also make provision for the co-option of either expert or Ex-officio board members in order to bring in skills which may be missing (even temporarily) from the skills capacity of the board as a whole. Such skills gaps may be discovered via a full Skills audit (see entry).

TUPE regulations

TUPE refers to the "Transfer of Undertakings (Protection of Employment) Regulations 2006" as amended by the "Collective Redundancies and Transfer of Undertakings (Protection of Employment) (Amendment) Regulations 2014". The TUPE rules apply to organisations of all sizes and protect employees' rights when the organisation or service they work for transfers to a new employer. The TUPE regulations apply if a business or part of a business moves to a new owner or merges with another business to make a brand new employer. They also apply when a contractor takes over activities from a client (known as outsourcing); when a new contractor takes over activities from another contractor (known as re-tendering); when a client takes over activities from a contractor (known as in sourcing).

Turnover

- The amount of money taken by a business in a particular period.
or
- The rate at which employees leave a workforce and are replaced.

Tweeting

The act of sending a message (a Tweet) on the social networking site Twitter - see entry below.

Twitter

An online social networking service and micro-blogging service created in 2006 that enables its users to send and read text-based messages of up to 140 characters, known as "tweets". Membership bodies use Twitter as part of their Social media strategy (see entry).

U

Ultra vires

A Latin term meaning 'beyond powers'. An act done outside of legal authority and could equally be termed invalid. Its opposite, i.e. an act done within legal authority, is valid or 'intra vires'.

Unfair dismissal

The term used in UK labour law to describe an employer's action when terminating an employee's employment contrary to the requirements of the Employment Rights Act 1996 and where the contract of employment has been terminated for unfair or inadmissible reasons. When challenged in court, the employer must establish that the dismissal was based on a substantial reason such as gross misconduct, lack of qualification, incapability to perform assigned duties or redundancy. In such cases, the courts usually take the employee's statutory rights into consideration.

Usability

Usability is a quality attribute that assesses how easy user interfaces are to use. The word usability also refers to methods for improving ease-of-use during the product or service design process, especially in terms of functionality by ensuring that it does it what users need.

User experience (UX)

User experience encompasses all aspects of the end-user's interaction with the organisation, its services, and its products. The international standard ISO 9241-210 (Ergonomics of human system interaction), defines user experience as "a person's perceptions and responses that result from the use or anticipated use of a product, system or service" and will, therefore, include all the users' emotions, beliefs, preferences, perceptions, physical and psychological responses, behaviours and accomplishments that occur before, during and after use.

User experience should be distinguished from Usability (see entry).

User representation

To offer the facility for users of the organisation's products and services to feedback on their experience and contribute to the quality of the products and services within a programme of ongoing improvement.

User statistics – see also Statistics

The collection, organisation, analysis, interpretation and presentation of data relating to use of an organisation's products and services by members as well as non-members.

User-testing

A technique used in user-centred interaction design to evaluate a product by testing it on users, focusing on measuring a product's capacity to meet its intended purpose.

USP (Unique selling proposition / Unique selling point)

A marketing concept first proposed as a theory to explain a pattern in successful advertising campaigns of the early 1940s. Such campaigns made unique propositions to the customer that convinced them to switch brands. Theodore Levitt, a professor at Harvard Business School, suggested that, "Differentiation is one of the most important strategic and tactical activities in which companies must constantly engage." The term has been used to describe an individual or organisation's personal brand in the marketplace.

V

Value-added or Affinity membership scheme
This type of scheme usually complements established membership schemes in order to offer increased member value. Schemes are either conducted internally or externally by commercial affinity providers. Benefits vary widely from High Street discounts to organisation-linked offers.

Value for money (VFM)
A term used to assess whether or not an organisation has obtained the maximum benefit from the goods and services it both acquires and provides, within the resources available to it.

Values – see also Mission statement, Vision and Objects
Ideas about the worth or importance of things, concepts and people.

VAT – Value added tax
A type of consumption tax that is placed on a product whenever value is added at a stage of production and at final sale. Value-added tax (VAT) is most often used in the European Union. The amount of value-added tax that the user pays is the cost of the product, less any of the costs of materials used in the product that have already been taxed.

VAT MOSS – VAT mini one stop shop
New EU VAT rules in effect from January 2015 change the place of supply in respect of all supplies of telecommunications, broadcasting and e-services to consumers from the place where the supplier is located to the place where the consumer resides. From this date, EU and non-EU business will have to register and account for VAT in every Member State in which they supply such services to consumers. HMRC (Her Majesty's Revenue & Customs) have set up VAT Moss which is a one stop shop to assist small organisations to pay VAT to European counterparts.

Venture capital
>Money provided by investors, especially to start-up firms and small businesses, with perceived long-term growth potential. This is a very important source of funding for start-ups that do not have access to capital markets. It typically entails high risk for the investor, but it has the potential for above-average returns.

Verifiable CPD - see also Continuing Professional Development
>This is the term given to often structured learning that can be evidenced, e.g. a certificate confirming attendance at a conference or participation in an eLearning course.

Vice-President - see President

Virtual learning environment (VLE) - see Online learning environment

Virtual member – see also Digital-only membership model
>A member whose benefits of membership of an organisation are delivered and used entirely in an online environment, e.g. electronic publications, emails, other electronic materials.

Vision / Vision statement – see also Mission Statement, Values and Objects
>An aspirational description of what an organisation would like to achieve or accomplish in the mid-term or long-term future. It is intended to serve as a clear guide for choosing current and future courses of action.
>
>A mission is different from a vision in that the former is the cause and the latter is the effect; a mission is something to be accomplished whereas a vision is something to be pursued for that accomplishment.

Voluntary sector
>The voluntary sector or community sector (also non-profit sector or not-for-profit sector) is the sphere of social activity undertaken by organisations that are not for profit and non-

governmental. This sector is also called the Third sector, in reference to the public sector and the private sector.

Volunteer agreement – see also Management of volunteers
Document taking the form of an agreed code of practice or contract between a volunteer and the organisation with which they are working, which dictates how the volunteer will contribute both time and effort on behalf of the organisation and its members.

Volunteerism
The policy or practice of volunteering one's time or talents for charitable, educational, or other worthwhile activities, especially in the community.

Volunteer – see Management of volunteers
A person who works for or on behalf of an organisation without being paid.

Voting - see also Membership category and Online voting
Full members are likely to have voting rights and so can vote in elections for Council or Committee members. Voting has traditionally been done via hard copy, however a growing number of organisations are enabling members to vote online and this is having a positive impact on participation.

W

Web analytics
>   The measurement, collection, analysis and reporting of internet data for purposes of understanding and optimising web usage

Website maximisation – see also Search engine optimisation (SEO)

Welcome pack
>   A set of documentation sent to the new member once the joining process is completed and payment has been received.

What-if analysis
>   The process of evaluating alternate strategies by answering the consequences of changes to the way a job, task, process might be changed.

Whistleblower policy – see also Employee protection
>   This policy is intended to encourage Board members, staff (paid and volunteer) and others to report suspected or actual occurrence(s) of illegal, unethical or inappropriate events (behaviours or practices) without fear of retribution.

Whiteboard syndrome
>   A form of employee malaise brought on by the overuse of whiteboards for meetings, often leading to particular employees monopolising the pen and the conversation and ultimately an inability of the group to make decisions.

White-label product or service
>   A product or service produced by one company (the producer) that other companies (the marketers) rebrand to make it appear as if they originally created it.

White paper
>   An authoritative report or guide helping readers to understand an issue, solve a problem, or make a decision. White papers

are used in two main spheres: government and business-to-business marketing.

WIFM principle (What's in it for me?)

This principle expresses the idea that most people will want to know how a situation or an idea will benefit them directly before acting on it or becoming involved. This question should be answered very clearly when recruiting or trying to retain volunteers.

Working group – see also Task group

A group of people working together temporarily until a specific goal is achieved and then usually disbanded.

X

x-Axis

> The axis on a graph that is usually drawn left to right and usually shows the range of values of an independent variable.

Y

y-Axis

> The axis on a graph that is usually drawn from bottom to top and usually shows the range of values of variable dependent on one other variable, or the second of two independent variables.

Young members

> A term which describes student members or young professionals at the beginning of their careers and who might be considered to have specific needs within any membership strategy which addresses 'cradle-to-grave' membership or where such members may dip in and out of membership over time.

Z

z-Axis

>   The axis on a graph that is usually drawn as if vertical and usually shows the range of values of a variable dependent on two other variables or the third independent variable.

Zen – see also Mindfulness

>   The word 'Zen' is Japanese and translates as absorption or meditative state. Like Mindfulness, it is about living in the moment and being focused on just one thing at a time, thereby giving you total concentration and better results. Often applied to meditation.

Zero Growth – see also Market saturation

>   A situation in which a product has either become diffused (distributed) within a market and growth is no longer possible or growth in sales or market penetration is no longer happening for other reasons.

Zip code

>   A system of postal codes used by the United States Postal Service (USPS) since 1963. Known in the UK as post codes.

Zip file

>   A zip file (.zip) may contain one or more files or folders that may have been compressed into a smaller archive. This compressed file is an archive file format that supports lossless data compression. A zipped file takes up less hard drive space and takes less time to transfer to another computer. To use a zipped file, it will need to be unzipped first.

ACKNOWLEDGEMENTS & QUALITY ASSURANCE

The definitions in this book have been drawn from a very wide range of specialist, print and online resources which we acknowledge with gratitude.

The jargon busted in this publication has been checked by a group of senior association and membership professionals to ensure the content is comprehensive, appropriate and correct. Their assistance has been invaluable for both quality assurance and extending the range of terms covered.

All definitions are current at time of going to press but we acknowledge that terminology evolves very quickly in the sector and so additions or changes may need to be made in future editions.

FURTHER HELP

For advice and assistance with governance, strategic, professional services, operational issues or senior staff mentoring please contact:

Susie Kay at The Professionalism Group
www.theprofessionalismgroup.co.uk
susiekay@theprofessionalismgroup.co.uk

The Professionalism Group
The Professionalism Group provides advice, consultancy and mentoring services to associations and membership organisations. We assist individuals with personal support and career progression as well as assisting organisations in their professionalism and best practice in order to ensure that the organisation enhances its success.

For advice and assistance with membership, marketing, communications and online change and development contact:

Richard Gott at MemberWise
www.memberwise.org.uk
richard.gott@memberwise.org.uk

The MemberWise Network
The MemberWise Network is a professional network of over 3,000 association and membership professionals. The network is the leading free-to-join resource for association and membership professionals in the UK and provides good practice information and advice, regular updates, conferences and events.

HOW TO SPOT A DINOSAUR, or How to Survive and Thrive in the Workplace

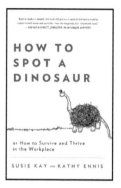

Available in paperback and as an e-book from Amazon,
PROFESSIONALISM BOOKS and all good bookshops

Realising that your friends and colleagues don't all operate the same way that you do can be an eye-opener. How to spot a Dinosaur is an effective and practical guide to understanding and managing your business and personal relationships.

This book helps you identify the different personality types around you and offers ways to deal with the difficulties in working with people who are unfamiliar to you or who don't see the world as you do. Inside you will find practical advice and strategies to help you stay in control of your workload, avoid too much stress and maintain your work-life balance. This inspiring book offers guidance in thinking about your career to date and where it might be leading you.

What do readers think of the book?

"Put simply, I believe this is excellent. If you plan to buy only one business-oriented book this year, make sure it's Dinosaur."

"A master class in understanding human nature, communication and the forces pervading issues which are not just about work issues but life issues as well."

"Love the language, prose and style, had me smiling regularly! A delightful read that is spot-on with describing characters often found in the workplace. Well done!! It must have taken a serious commitment to put it all together so well."

MAKE A NOTE OF ANY MISSING DEFINITIONS

For inclusion in the next edition of The Jargon Buster, send them to:

susiekay@theprofessionalismgroup.co.uk

Printed in Great Britain
by Amazon